THE CATHOLIC CHURCH
AND SCIENCE

THE CATHOLIC CHURCH AND SCIENCE

Answering the Questions, Exposing the Myths

Benjamin Wiker

TAN Books

Charlotte, North Carolina

ISBN: 978-0-89555-910-4

Cover design by Tony Pro.

Printed and bound in the United States of America.

TAN Books
Charlotte, North Carolina
2011

*To my wife and children, who
are more dear to me every day.*

ACKNOWLEDGMENTS

I WOULD like to thank, first of all, the Gallaghers for taking on this project, and Todd for shepherding me through it. And of course, I am grateful to my wife and children who patiently endured the many hours of reading and writing that went into making this book.

CONTENTS

A SHORT BUT VERY
IMPORTANT INTRODUCTION

G. K. Chesterton once famously described the Church as a carefully balanced chariot careening through history:

People have fallen into a foolish habit of speaking of orthodoxy as something heavy, humdrum, and safe. There never was anything so perilous or so exciting as orthodoxy. It was sanity: and to be sane is more dramatic than to be mad. It was the equilibrium of a man behind madly rushing horses, seeming to stoop this way and to sway that, yet in every attitude having the grace of statuary and the accuracy of arithmetic. The Church in its early days went fierce and fast with any warhorse . . . She swerved to the left and right, so exactly as to avoid enormous obstacles. She left on one hand the huge bulk of Arianism, buttressed by all the worldly powers to make Christianity too worldly. The next instant she was swerving to avoid an orientalism, which would have made it too unworldly. The orthodox Church never took the tame course or accepted the conventions; the orthodox Church was never respectable. It would have been easier to have accepted the Earthly power of the Arians. It would have been easy, in the Calvinistic seventeenth century, to fall into the bottomless pit of predestination. It is always easy to let the age have its head; the difficult thing is to keep one's own. It is always easy to be a modernist;

as it is easy to be a snob. To have fallen into any of those open traps of error and exaggeration which fashion after fashion and sect after sect set along the historic path of Christendom—that would indeed have been simple. It is always simple to fall; there are an infinity of angles at which one falls, only one at which one stands. To have fallen into any one of the fads from Gnosticism to Christian Science would indeed have been obvious and tame. But to have avoided them all has been one whirling adventure; and in my vision the heavenly chariot flies thundering through the ages, the dull heresies sprawling and prostrate, the wild truth reeling but erect.[1]

I don't expect to be understood, at this early point in the book, when I say that Chesterton has here captured, in some important senses, the truth about the relationship of the Catholic Church to science. It may seem a startling suggestion, because we don't think of science as somehow partaking of the strange vagaries and varieties of "fashion" and "sect" that one finds in the history of Christianity or the history of philosophy. And we certainly don't think of the Church as a charioteer swinging madly, left and right, to avoid *scientific* heresies. Unlike Chesterton's heavenly chariot, which lurches and reels through history, science, we are told, is a stately and stable omnibus taking humanity on a straight path from darkness to light, from superstition and ignorance to truth. Whereas the Church, we are also told, is something like a bedraggled old man on a donkey—at first clumsily and stupidly getting in the way of the omnibus of science, and then, once it has sped past, clumping sulkily behind.

Against all expectations, then, I will be making the case that Chesterton's vision of the Church as a chariot swerving to avoid errors to the left and right is also an entirely appropriate image of the Catholic Church's relationship to science. The difference is that whereas in regard to doctrinal orthodoxy the Church is immediately concerned with weeding out truth from heresy, in regard to science it is *mediately* concerned with weeding out falsehood from truth.

To avoid a misunderstanding here, I state plainly that the Church does not dictate the substance and detail of the various sciences. But for that matter, neither do the scientists. The particular reality under consideration determines the substance and details of each science, and thence judges the truth or falsehood of human scientific conjectures. The entomologist is not in the seat of ultimate authority; rather, the insects themselves have the last say in sorting out truth from falsehood in the entomologist's theories. The stars themselves will declare which astronomers are orthodox and which are heretics. The Earth has ultimate say against any geologist, no matter how prestigious. Nature itself, in all its profound complexity and mystery, is the ultimate authority over scientists.

But if the Church does not dictate the substance or the detail of any of the sciences, it watches with great care the proper parameters of the sciences and the general (and sometimes particular and peculiar) assumptions of the scientists. Here it must judge, and the reason is both simple and profound. Scientists are human, and sometimes the Church must step in to remind them of their limits, especially those limits that safeguard their own humanity (just as, in regard to Christian orthodoxy, the Church stepped in to safeguard both Christ's divinity and His humanity).

Let's take an important case to make the point more clear. As Chesterton noted, the Church intervened against John Calvin's doctrine of predestination. Calvin was so enamored of God's omniscience and omnipotence that he asserted that God created human beings already having determined who would be damned. Since one's eternal destiny in Heaven or Hell was thus laid out before one even existed, there wasn't anything that could be done to change it. One's actions were therefore of no (eternal) consequence. If this were true, the result would be both the ruin of our everyday experience of choosing to do or not do good and evil actions, and the casting away of the entire corpus of New Testament admonitions by Jesus Christ to do certain things in order to gain eternal life and to not do certain things in order to avoid eternal damnation. Calvinistic predestination made a hash of human action, both in regard to our experience of natural, everyday life, and in regard to revealed, supernatural truths about the relationship of our actions to our eternal destiny. The Church, even while mightily affirming God's omniscience and omnipotence, swerved away from Calvin and went hurtling onward.

But in modernity, a new kind of natural doctrine of predestination arose, championed by the scientific and philosophical materialists: those who argued that all of reality could be reduced to bits or clumps of inanimate matter, generally called atoms. The materialists denied the existence of the soul and proclaimed that all matter was subject to eternal laws that determined all motion. Our common, everyday experience of freely choosing our actions was illusory, for even our choosing was the result of the microscopic internal atomic motion of our bodies that was, as all things material, predestined by the laws of nature.

This heresy is still with us. It denies our experience of choosing, of having free will, and therefore, exactly like Calvin's heresy, makes hash of human action and nonsense of morality. And so the Church has swerved away from this "scientific" heresy, which is still in fashion even after 500 years, and condemned materialism and determinism, even while heartily affirming the study of the wonders of nature in astronomy, physics, chemistry, and biology.

Likewise, the Church has always rejected pantheism—also popular in modernity, especially among philosophers and physicists—wherein God is collapsed into nature and nature into God. The Church has done so for the doctrinal reason that Scripture reveals in Genesis, quite clearly, that God and nature are entirely distinct as Creator and creation, and also for the obvious natural reason that the Earth and the stars aren't gods (no matter what ancient or modern pagans dream to the contrary).

So the Church does, in important respects, sit in judgment of the sciences, steering its flock away from scientific theories that, however attractive and popular they may be, ultimately undermine natural and supernatural truths.

The Church as Patron

But that is not the only relationship the Church has with the sciences. While sitting as judge, the Church has also been a great *patron* of the sciences (and many prominent scientists have been Catholics). There are two reasons for this, and they are often intertwined.

The first may come as a bit of a surprise, so much so that I'll quote a secular historian as my authority. In *The Sun in the Church*, J. L. Heilbron begins, "The Roman Catholic Church gave more financial and social support to the study of astronomy for over six centuries, from the recovery of ancient learning in the late Middle Ages into the Enlightenment, than any other, and, probably, all other, institutions. Those who infer the Church's attitude from its persecution of Galileo may be reassured to know that the basis of its generosity to astronomy was not a love of science but a problem in administration. The problems were establishing and promulgating the date of Easter."[2] I quote the whole passage—barb about Galileo and all—to help make a rather difficult point. We are under the mistaken impression, given the omnipresence of active scientists and scientific institutions in our own day, that science just naturally happens, like a snowball rolling downhill gathers speed and bulk.

The truth is otherwise. The activity of science is more like pushing a large rock uphill—it is hard, dirty, tedious, and painful. Even the smallest of advances are 99 percent perspiration. Here on the other side of the light bulb's invention, things seem quite easy. We just click the light on, and take it for granted. But if we had struggled through all the painful, back-breaking, eye-straining hours with Thomas Edison to get the first light bulb to work, we would understand a lot more about the mental and physical mountain he had to climb just to set a single luminescent globe at the top of his efforts.[3]

Just so with all the great advances in science, they took immense physical struggle and enormous mental effort. They were also expensive and in many instances were only possible because of significant patronage. The case mentioned earlier of the Church's six-century support of astronomy is an excellent illustration of the way that the advance of science and the advancement of the Church went hand in hand historically.

Another important example of patronage, as we'll see in a later chapter, was the Church's development of the universities in the Middle Ages, which formed the intellectual foundations of modern science. Of course, we have the obvious ongoing contributions made by the various science departments in Catholic universities around the world. And we might mention that one of the finest astronomical observatories in the world is the Vatican Observatory.

But let us return to Heilbron's point, for it allows us to understand an interesting and important way that the Church advanced science. The problem of Easter is actually a problem of sorting out natural time: if the sun always stood directly overhead and there were no visible stars or moon and no seasons, our sense of time would be almost undeveloped. But as it is, there are wonderful natural regularities that serve to mark things off. The sun rises and sets, marking off the days; the moon rises and sets and runs through its phases, marking off months; the seasons change, marking off years. The problem, however, is that the natural division of a month as marked by the lunar cycle, the natural division of the day as marked by the sun, and the natural division of a year as marked by the seasons, don't quite line up with each other. Things get more difficult if you pick a special day—say, the

Jewish Passover—and try to set it by the lunar month, and even more difficult if you are a universal Church trying to set your Easter date by the Jewish Passover.

The Church's deep, supernaturally inspired desire to set the exact date of Easter led it to devote enormous resources, monetary and intellectual, toward making precise astronomical observations that probed the most dizzying details of mathematics, physics, and architecture. This desire led them to build cathedrals that would pinpoint the exact date of of Easter, by letting in a shaft of sunlight that would reveal, on the carefully calibrated floor, the solution to the problem. The cathedrals represent, concretely, a unity of beauty and truth, both natural and supernatural, all of which is aimed at the celebration of the Mass. Science, we might say, both served worship and benefitted from it. It is a historical fact, then, that the Church was at times a great patron of natural science so that it could be precise about supernatural matters.

But we've also uncovered another reason for its patronage, and this too is a matter of orthodoxy. The Church, from the very earliest days, reeled away from prominent heretics who declared that the physical world was made by an evil god. The Old Testament, in Genesis, declared otherwise: that the Earth was a good creation of a good Creator. Moreover, the Psalmists proclaimed that creation sings the glory of its Creator and shines forth His wisdom. If that weren't enough, in the New Testament, Jesus Christ Himself was revealed to be truly (created) man as well as truly (uncreated) God, so the Church had doubly to affirm that the order of nature, nature itself, declares the wisdom of God. Investigating the wisdom of God in nature was not only permissible but good. Knowing more about nature meant knowing more about God's wisdom manifested in creation.

And so, in celebrating the supernatural mystery of the Resurrection, the Church was at the same time celebrating the glorious intricacies of nature it had come to know in greater detail in its efforts to unlock the mysteries of time. It therefore rejoices in two kinds of truth: those revealing the wisdom of God the Creator and those revealing the love of God the Redeemer. It has no anxiety about raising a single voice in the double praise, because the Creator God and the Redeemer God are the same God.

The Church's Position in Regard to Science

The Church, then, has both a negative and positive relationship to science. It is both a judge protecting the truth and a patron supporting the discovery of truth. Both relationships are essential, and we'll see both illustrated in the chapters to come.

We end this introduction with a summary of the relationship between faith and science as offered in the *Catechism of the Catholic Church* (which is itself a compilation of previous statements given by the Church).

> Though faith is above reason, there can never be any real discrepancy between faith and reason. Since the same God who reveals mysteries and infuses faith has bestowed the light of reason on the human mind, God cannot deny himself, nor can truth ever contradict truth.
>
> Consequently, methodical research in all branches of knowledge, provided it is carried out in a truly scientific manner and does not override moral laws, can never conflict with the faith, because the things of the world and the things of faith derive from the same God. The humble and persevering investigator of the secrets of nature is being led, as it were, by the hand of God in spite of himself, for it is God, the conserver of all things, who made them what they are. (para. 159)

Science *cannot conflict with revelation* because the God who creates is the same as the God who redeems. Seeming contradictions between science and faith, however, can arise.

How do seeming contradictions arise? On the side of science, we must realize that human beings are profoundly human, and so human scientists can and do put forth a lot of wrong-headed theories. A humble investigator is one who knows his own limitations, one who understands that scientific effort is often skewed by human sin, simple miscalculation, confusion, philosophical error, and political ideology; therefore, the humble investigator is one who is open to correction. The history of science is littered with discarded theories, any one of which was held by the preeminent scientists of the day. That in itself is cause for scientific humility, and also a warning against those who impatiently and imprudently push the Church to conform its truths to the latest scientific fad.

On the side of faith, since the God of nature and the God of revelation are the same God, the Church holds that the secrets of nature that science slowly and humbly uncovers cannot contradict revelation. Therefore if our grasp of biblical revelation, for instance, ever seemed out of sorts with what science legitimately reveals—if the Earth were proved to be several billion years old, in apparent contradiction to the revealed data in Genesis—then we could be assured that God the Creator is not trying to contradict Himself in revelation. Rather, we are being happily pressed to understand that revelation in a deeper way.

Of course, these are rather bare-bone statements. The following chapters will give them flesh as we sort out the most prominent and pervasive confusions that have arisen in regard to the way that the Church relates to science and science to the Church. As the little barb about Galileo quoted earlier in this introduction reminds us, there are many who are quite skeptical that what we've just outlined represents how the Church has *actually* dealt with science over the centuries. So we have two kinds of confusion (at least!) to clear up: confusion that results from our not having enough information (and so the need to flesh things out) and confusion that results from misinformation (and so the need to set things straight). Very often, we'll find the two kinds of confusion mixed together, therefore compounding the problems we face in sorting things out.

I propose, then, to look at seven areas of common confusion, to supply information where it is lacking, and to correct misinformation where it is present in the hope of providing greater understanding about the true and proper relationship of the Catholic Church to science.

THE FIRST CONFUSION

"The Catholic Church Is at War with Science (and Faith Is at War with Reason)"

The whole point of this book is to make clear the relationship of the Catholic Church to science, and from what we've seen in the introduction, that relationship should be harmonious. Now, to many, this seems an odd and even laughable notion, as I just recently experienced.

The day before I wrote these very words, I was doing a radio interview and at the end the interviewer asked, "What book are you working on now?" I replied that I was working on a book about the relationship of the Catholic Church to science. "Oh, that should be interesting," he said, after an embarrassing on-air pause, "I know they've . . . uh . . . always been engaged in conflict."

Ah, confusion!—and obviously the one we've got to make some effort to clear up first. After all, if it's true that the Church and science have always been at war, then regardless of what either I or the *Catechism* says about their potential harmony, the facts of history speak otherwise. So in this chapter we'll look at the origin of the myth of the great and ongoing war between science and Christianity, the myth that colors the vision of all too many people (including some Catholics, no doubt). This myth is also part of a larger confused belief: that reason itself and faith are fundamentally opposed. This, too, we shall investigate.

The Myth That Science and Christianity Are at War

Undoubtedly the most persistent myth about the relationship of science to religion in general, and to Catholicism in particular, is that they have always been, are now, and will forever be locked in fundamental antagonism. This myth distorts our understanding of history, especially when it guides historians. One of the most distorted of all histories, and also one of the most influential, was John William Draper's *History of the Conflict between Religion and Science*, published in 1874.

Draper was born in England in 1811 but immigrated to America in 1832. He was an extraordinary scientist, making fundamental contributions to chemistry, astronomy, botany, medicine, and the development and scientific use of photography. But he is most remembered for his *History of the Conflict between Religion and Science*, and it was extremely influential in forming our academic and popular versions of the "warfare myth."

As work in the history of science over the last quarter-century has clearly shown, although Draper was certainly an excellent scientist, as an historian of the relationship of the Church to science he was a mere anti-Catholic propagandist.[1] Part of the book's authority rested on Draper's considerable scientific achievements. How could such a smart man, and such a good scientist, not be right about everything he said? We should add that the other source of his book's authority was external: the pervading climate of antagonism toward the Church in an increasingly secular age. People—some people anyway—wanted to hear exactly what Draper so passionately wanted to say, and so they treated his work as authoritative.

But Draper wasn't the first to air the warfare myth. Just before him, Andrew Dickson White, the founder of Cornell University, had fired off a now-famous public lecture, "The Battle-Fields of Science," that was published in the *New York Daily Tribune* on December 18, 1869. Not content with this first salvo, White would later hammer out a two-volume compendium of the sins of Christianity against science, *A History of the Warfare of Science with Theology in Christendom* (1896). To be fair to White, he believed that science was only in conflict with "dogmatic theology" rather than religion per se (although White's notion of religion "pure and undefiled" simply meant Christianity stripped of all dogmatic content, which meant that it was no longer Christianity). And no institution, in White's eyes, could have been more dogmatic than the Catholic Church.

But we've not yet gotten back to the origin of the warfare myth. White's overall historical thesis, that there was an essential conflict "between two epochs in the evolution of human thought—the theological and the scientific"[2]—was more or less a repetition of an earlier philosophical argument made by French philosopher Auguste Comte (1798–1857) that history is necessarily and inevitably moving through three distinct epochs: the theological, the metaphysical, and the scientific (or positivist). Or to put it another way, history was moving from religious superstition to philosophy and finally to hard science. For the sake of progress, science *must* replace religion.

Comte was not original either, but was simply codifying the Radical Enlightenment notion, running all the way back to the 17th century, that a new age of reason had dawned and it was time to throw off the chains of religion and of Catholicism in particular. The barely closeted atheist Thomas Hobbes provided a particularly animated attack on the Catholic Church in his *Leviathan* (1651), calling it the source of intellectual darkness because its belief in the immaterial soul and spirits (buttressed by the "vain philosophy" of Aristotle) was an obstacle to acceptance of the materialism Hobbes championed as the proper foundation of the new science.[3]

As the number of adherents to philosophical materialism grew, antagonism to religion (especially Catholicism) grew with it. This *philosophical* materialism formed the foundation of a new *scientific* materialism: the dubious philosophical view that to be reasonable means to affirm that material reality is the only reality came to define science itself. To be scientific meant to be a materialist and since materialism denies spiritual realities, to be scientific thus meant to deny that a purely spiritual God exists, that human beings have souls, and that souls live on after death in a state of bliss or damnation. Such is the ultimate source of modern science's secular and secularizing bent, which both fed and fed on the myth that the Church is at war.

By the time we get to the 18th century, the so-called Age of Enlightenment, the myth was widespread among intellectual movers and shakers. To note an important example, Paul Henri Thierry Baron d'Holbach (1723–89) united unabated materialism with undisguised atheism. D'Holbach included among his radical Enlightenment circle such luminaries as Jean-Jacques Rousseau, Benjamin Franklin, Adam Smith, and David Hume.

In his famous *System of Nature* (1770), d'Holbach asserted a fundamental animosity between religion and man's natural good. "The source of man's unhappiness is his ignorance of Nature," declared d'Holbach on the very first page.[4] Man is solely "the work of nature.—He exists in Nature.—He is submitted to the laws of Nature.—He cannot deliver himself from them," he then declared, the point being that there is nothing outside material nature.[5] Our alienation from our natural selves began with the rise of religion, when our eyes and efforts were turned from this world to some imaginary next world. Materialist science signals a return to the study of nature as the sole arena of truth, which will cure us of our alienation from our natural good.

D'Holbach's view makes for an obvious historical antipathy: science takes us forward to happiness and salvation; religion drags us backward into alienation, ignorance, and superstition. It's easy to see how d'Holbach's scheme, entirely derived from his materialist assumptions, could provide the framework for subsequent histories of the relationship of science to religion in the 19th century, such as we've seen with Draper and White. But again, this idea wasn't original to him; he merely elaborated the basic, radical Enlightenment notion that religion and reason, the supernatural and the natural, were locked in fundamental antagonism.

Here we return to an essential point about history-telling: the relationship between one's predilections and one's research. If a particular historian disdains religion and is convinced that religion is infantile or pernicious, worship of God is foolish superstition, religion makes us unhappy, all priests are frauds, and religion is the cause of all wars, then he will naturally gather all possible instances of religion's seeming to be infantile, having pernicious consequences, entailing foolish superstition, and causing misery, and he will also comb out occurrences of fraudulent priests and religious wars. Much of the evidence will be quite real—original sin is an essential Christian doctrine—but much will be a distortion, and much that would count in favor of religion will be entirely ignored.

We can understand how the Enlightenment's antagonism toward religion would produce a history of science like Draper's and White's, which *seemed* to show that science and religion have always been in essential conflict—with materialist science being the beacon of light and religion the foul, resistant power of darkness. It is largely the result of gathering only the evidence that fits the assumption and arguing for that assumption as if it were a conclusion.

If, on the other hand, these assumptions are dropped, and evidence is gathered without bias, a much different picture of the relationship of religion to science emerges. We know this from the last quarter-century of fresh research into the history of science, wherein historians have accumulated mounds of evidence that contradict the Draper-White warfare thesis (and we'll incorporate the new material into our subsequent chapters).

Yet, all this having been said, we can also see that there is *some* truth in the view that there is a certain kind of antagonism between Christianity and modern science. Insofar as many proponents of modern science have been doctrinaire materialists, there has been conflict, for materialism and Christianity *are* at essential odds, and must always remain so. We should not, then, be surprised that as adherence to materialism has grown and spread, antagonism both to and from Christianity has increased. Materialism by definition excludes any immaterial reality. Christianity by definition cannot abide this exclusion. But the notion—running from Thomas Hobbes down through the Radical Enlightenment to Draper and White and on to the present day—that history demonstrates complete antipathy between Christianity and science is a myth that is as pernicious as it is false.

The Belief That Faith and Reason Are in Essential Antagonism

The idea that reason and faith are fundamentally antagonistic is also a myth, but it too has some basis in reality. Just as there have been some conflicts between Christianity and science, there have been some Christians (often called "fideists") who have declared that faith (Latin, "*fides*") is indeed irrational and some scientists who have been happy to agree. But Catholicism rejects fideism and affirms the powers of human reason, even while recognizing that our use of reason is limited and tainted by sin.

That last point deserves some emphasis and explanation. It is often assumed that, since the Church places faith above reason and asserts that human reason is both limited and affected by sin, it is opposing faith to reason as if the two were at war. Nothing could be further from the truth, as Pope John Paul II made clear in his initial greeting in the encyclical *Fides et Ratio* (*Faith and Reason*): "Faith and reason are like two wings on which the human spirit rises to the contemplation of truth; and God has placed in the human heart a desire to know the truth—in a word, to know himself—so that, by knowing and loving God, men and women may also come to the fullness of truth about themselves."[6] So far from denigrating reason against faith, the Church heartily affirms that reason helps us rise to the contemplation of God. Science, properly understood and exercised, can unveil truths about God through his work of creation. Again, the activity of science is affirmed by the Church's insistence that the God of Creation and the God of Revelation are one God.

The distinction between faith and reason, then, is not between the irrational and rational, but between the humanly unknowable and the humanly knowable. We can understand this distinction even on the natural level. For most of us, there is a big gap between what we can understand and what we accept on the authority of someone more knowledgeable (at least in a particular area). I look up from my computer to my office wall, on which hangs a poster of the periodic table of elements with all its nice, neat rows of chemical symbols from hydrogen to ununoctium. The order of the periodic table is really pretty easy to understand: each successive element has one more proton in the nucleus (accounting for its horizontal order), and the electrons fall into definite structural patterns in "shells" orbiting the nucleus (accounting for its vertical order). The overall structure is easy enough for my limited scientific and mathematical mind to understand that I've even written a book about its historical development—aimed at kids between 12 and 16 (*The Mystery of the Periodic Table*).

But there is a big gap between my understanding and that of a world-class chemist. Until I come to understand the chemical world from the inner experience of an expert chemical theoretician and to grasp the mathematics entailed in quantum mechanics—which is unlikely to happen—my knowledge of chemistry, beyond a certain, very limited point, must come from information accepted on faith. I must trust in the truths that scientists and mathematical physicists reveal to me, for what they know is beyond my own natural, rational powers to understand. But what they reveal, although above my reason, does not contradict what I have come to know about chemistry by my own reason; rather, it completes it and corrects it, taking it above where it could naturally reach. Likewise, the Church says that there are truths beyond the powers of *all* human reason, and that there is a being, God, whose intellect far surpasses our own, who *does* know them, and whose knowledge, revealed by faith, corrects and completes our own.

This would seem to be quite a reasonable explanation. So where did it come from, this all-too-common notion that faith and reason are in conflict? We've already seen one source in the modern world. Modern materialist thinkers like Hobbes assumed that to be reasonable meant to accept materialism, and since the Church rejected materialism, then, so the logic goes, faith must be irrational.

But there is another source: the Reformation, which broke apart the unity of Christendom and ended in the religious wars of the 17th century. Those religio-political conflicts led certain influential figures to assume that faith, especially Christian faith, is doubly irrational because Christians cannot come to rational agreement about their faith, and because their disagreement leads to irrational bloodshed. Against the disorders and confusions of faith, these "enlightened" figures set the glorious harmony of reason: the universal source of light and peaceful agreement, and therefore the beacon by which we can progress beyond religious-based confusion and conflict to a brave, new world of rational, secular peace.

Ah yes, the warfare thesis again! The problem with the warfare thesis as applied to the relationship of faith and reason is that it's still false. To begin with, we should note that many who hold the notion that faith and reason are at war often assume that reason is *not* at war with itself. We should not be surprised to find that this assumption was particularly strong in the 18th-century

Enlightenment. Reason is universal, Enlightenment *philosophes* declared confidently, and necessarily yields universal agreement. Religion, which is irrational, yields confusion and hence intractable diversity and political conflict.

So the Enlightenment story went. But history tells a different story about the fate of reason left to itself. In the ancient world, there were nearly as many philosophical sects, with their rival subdivisions, as there were philosophers—the Sophists, the followers of Democritus, Pythagoras, Heraclitus, Plato, Aristotle, and Epicurus, the Academic skeptics, the Stoics, Cynics, and Eclectics. Reason, independent of faith, does not easily lead to happy uniformity, but rather, quite often to division.

From its inception forward, modernity is even more fractured. Neo-Pythagoreans claimed that the world was entirely mathematical and neo-Epicureans that it was entirely material. Skeptics like Pierre Bayle attacked the power of reason and naïve rationalists like the early Deists defended it. Cartesians exalted a mathematical-deductive theoretical science and Baconian empiricists denied the validity of it. Idealists like Bishop Berkeley preached that the mind determined the world and materialists like Hobbes countered that the mind is determined by matter. Spiritualists like Georg Hegel saw God manifesting himself in history and positivists like Auguste Comte saw history as manifesting the end of religion. Logical positivists thought that the driest reason could solve all problems and existentialists and nihilists thought that faith in reason itself was the problem. Sophisticated rationalists like Immanuel Kant drew a host of disciples, but then, so did sophisticated antirationalists like Friedrich Nietzsche.

There is, to put it kindly, an embarrassment of riches among both ancient and modern philosophers that should make it clear that reason by itself does not yield easy uniformity. Thus, it is no decisive point against faith that Christians have exhibited serious disagreements and fallen into rival sects. The same thing happens among secular philosophers.

The obvious conclusion to draw from this historical philosophical diversity is the Catholic one: that even though it is wonderful, human reason is merely human. We are not omniscient gods, and our reason is fallible; the more deeply we think about things, the more difficult it is to sort them out. Indeed, recognition of the fallibility and limitations of human reason is itself quite rational, for its fallibility and limitations are historically well-documented. In fact, in modernity, it was the recognition of the fallibility and limitations of reason that led philosophers from the unfounded optimism in the powers of reason in the 18th-century Enlightenment to the complete pessimism about reason among the late 20th- and 21st-century existentialists and nihilists.

The Catholic Church recognizes reason's value and its limits and so steers clear of unfounded optimism in reason on the one side and ungrounded skepticism against reason on the other. The Church therefore guards against proponents of both philosophical extremes: the heady rationalist who foolishly believes that human reason, in fact, can and does know everything, as if we were gods, and the nearly headless skeptic who denies that reason can know anything at all, as if we were brute beasts.

But the realization that human reason is fallible and limited is, in an important way, an acknowledgment of the possibility and desirability of faith, for it recognizes that it would be very helpful for our reason (to say the least) if an infallible and unlimited intellectual being would reveal either the truths that we cannot reach by our own powers (and so we would have to hold them on trust, i.e., by faith) or truths that we are inclined to lose or distort through our own foolishness or wickedness (and so we must accept as a disciplinary corrective). It would also be quite rational to assume that the truths revealed above reason would have to be protected from attack and confusion from below.

The Church as Patron and Protector of Reason and Faith

Pope John Paul II's words from *Fides et Ratio* help sum up our points in this section as well as advance our understanding further.

> The Church has no philosophy of her own nor does she canonize any one particular philosophy in preference to others . . . At the deepest level, the autonomy which philosophy enjoys is rooted in the fact that reason is by its nature oriented to truth and is equipped moreover with the means necessary to arrive at truth.
>
> Yet history shows that philosophy—especially modern philosophy—has taken wrong turns and fallen into error. It is neither the task nor the competence of the Magisterium to intervene in order to make good the lacunas of deficient philosophical discourse. Rather, it is the Magisterium's duty to respond clearly and strongly when controversial philosophical opinions threaten right understanding of what has been revealed, and when partial theories which sow the seed of serious error, confusing the pure and simple faith of the People of God, begin to spread more widely.[7]

To avoid being vague, the Pope then named several "philosophical presuppositions and conclusions . . . incompatible with revealed truth."[8] Here again, the Church has veered away from extremes, setting itself against "all forms of rationalism" that denied revealed truths above reason, and against "the temptations of fideism" that denied the importance of reason. It has steered away from "radical traditionalism" for distrusting reason and "ontologism" for trusting it too much. It has rejected historicism for making all truth merely historical, evolutionism for making all truth merely biological, and existentialism for denying that there was any metaphysical foundation to claims of truth; for all of these, in rejecting reason's ability to truly know things, were rejecting even the possibility of science. The Church has thrown out Marxism for reducing human beings, including their very thoughts, to mere reflections of economic conditions, and disallowed "Biblicism" because it "tends to make the reading and exegesis of Sacred Scripture the sole criterion of truth."[9]

We needn't go into the details of any of these errors. We should note, however, that some of them are philosophical and some theological; that is, some have to do with reason and some with faith. As we noted previously, the Church exercises the same critical stance toward both. It isn't "faith against reason," or "faith against science," but *truth against falsehood*, wherever it appears. As with philosophy—if we might slightly alter the words of John Paul II—it is not "the task nor the competence of the Magisterium to intervene in order to make good the lacunas of deficient scientific discourse" by attempting to judge or correct particular experiments or aspects of theories. But as with philosophy, it must watch over the deepest assumptions, general contours, and larger conclusions.

This is preeminently the case where a particular philosophy deeply informs the assumptions and practices of particular sciences, as has been the case with materialist philosophy. So for example, as we shall see in a later chapter, the Church does not object to the theory of evolution but only to a strictly materialist understanding of evolution. It doesn't object to chemistry, but only to the materialist notion that everything can be reduced to chemicals.

An Additional Warning

As historian of science Noah Efron smartly states, "For every myth there is an equal and opposite myth."[10] While we might not want to call it a "myth," it is true that a certain kind of reaction to the warfare thesis has occurred among Christians who, tired of the drubbing given to the Faith by the secularists, are zealous to show that Christianity was actually *the* source, *the* cause of modern science. It's not difficult to understand how this reaction arose. When historians sifted through the great mound of evidence, reaching way back into the Middle Ages, that had been neglected by the Drapers and Whites, they began to recover the full extent to which Christians had contributed to the rise of modern science. To some of them (especially to irritated Christians), it was as natural to overplay the evidence as it had been for secular materialists to ignore it.

The general argument goes something like this: "Modern science was born in a particular culture, a Christian culture, and we can trace its antecedents backward all the way into the early Middle Ages. No other culture—Greek, Roman, Indian, Chinese, Egyptian, Babylonian, Islamic, African, Mayan—ever gave us anything like modern science. Therefore, the cause of modern science's success must lie, ultimately, in Christianity, and the more we dig into the Christian origins of modern science, the farther back we find positive evidence for the sustained, sophisticated developments that underlay modern science."

In the early 20th century, the French Catholic Pierre Duhem (1861–1916), a physicist, mathematician, and philosopher and historian of science, showed decisively that the Catholic Middle Ages were not a dark time but contained an essential storehouse of riches contributing to the development of natural philosophy, mathematics, logic, and experiment, leading up to modern science. His ten-volume *The System of the World: A History of Cosmological Doctrines from Plato to Copernicus* would have been more than enough to sink Draper's thesis since it demonstrated that modern science depended on previous developments made possible by the Catholic Church in the Middle Ages.

There were others who recognized Christianity's important

contributions to science. In a more general way, the philosopher Alfred North Whitehead (1861–1947) confirmed much the same claim as Duhem, asserting that "the greatest contribution of medievalism to the formation of the scientific movement" was "the inexpugnable belief that every detailed occurrence can be correlated with its antecedents in a perfectly definite manner, exemplifying general principles." What made modern science even *possible* was "the medieval insistence on the rationality of God, conceived as with the personal energy of Jehovah and with the rationality of a Greek philosopher. Every detail was supervised and ordered: the search into nature could only result in the vindication of the faith in rationality."[11] Without Christianity, the argument goes, the belief in an intrinsic order of nature would not have occurred, and this belief was necessary for the advent of modern science.

A more restricted version of this approach, now famous as the Merton Thesis, was offered by Robert Merton (1910–2003), who alleged that it was, in fact, the peculiarities of English Puritanism in the 17th century that gave the decisive boost to modern science. Although Merton's thesis was attractive to Protestants, it has the obvious defects entailed in ignoring or severely downplaying all the contributions to modern science made by non-Englishmen and Catholics (especially the Jesuits) and the wealth of scientific development that had occurred from the early Middle Ages up to the 17th century.

Much has been done since the first half of the 20th century in the history of science to vindicate the essential contributions that Christianity has made to it, helping to reveal, hence show, the glaring defects of warfare myth.[12] But as the most recent studies also stress, we can't assume the opposite as true—that Christianity, or Catholicism or Protestantism alone, is responsible for the advent of modern science—without distorting what really happened.

To begin with, it simply isn't true to insist that Christianity alone gave birth to the notion of an ordered, intelligible universe. That notion was found in Greek and Roman pagan thought, and it is impossible to trace the origins of modern science very far without running into the enormous influence of Plato, Pythagoras, Aristotle, the Stoics, Euclid, Ptolemy, and Galen. We must also include the significant contributions made through Islam, not just accidentally as a mediator of Greek texts to the Latin West, but essentially, adding definite substance.[13]

Moreover, even while Christianity was playing its significant part, there was a renewal of pagan ideas that directly challenged Christianity but were fruitfully used to advance aspects of modern science. To cite the obvious: revived forms of pagan materialism, especially those offered by the ancient Greek atomists Democritus and Epicurus, fueled interest in studying the material details of the natural world. Materialism, even though fundamentally erroneous, did lead to genuine advances in the sciences, and some of those contributors no doubt embraced materialism precisely because materialistically defined science would help to vindicate an anti-Christian world view.[14]

Nor can we leave out the importance for modern science of the renewed interest in magic during the Renaissance and beyond. "Magic adepts" were passionately interested in controlling nature through knowledge of her secrets.[15] Their passion led to discovery. For much the same reason, the long-standing interest in alchemy, dating back to the ancient world but gaining steam in both the Renaissance and Enlightenment, was essential to the modern advance of medicine, chemistry, physics, meteorology, metallurgy, and geology.[16] We also cannot forget the enormous push in early modern astronomy that came from the dubious desire to cast ever more accurate astrological horoscopes.[17] It would be hard to tag these as essentially Christian, for in fact, the spirit behind them was often quite heterodox.

There are also quite natural causes of the advance of science, such as the obvious and very human characteristics found in Christians and non-Christians alike. For example, natural human curiosity, the desire for fame or wealth, a nation's schemes for empire or conquest, the culinary enchantments of sugar, coffee, and spices, all advanced the science of navigation. And the list goes on. Although many Christians, being human, have been part of these advances, it is difficult to make the case that these contributing causes are specifically Christian. And so, we cannot accept the notion that Christianity is *the* cause of modern science.

The Position of the Church

The Catholic Church rejects the two myths and too-zealous reaction to them and does so for central doctrinal reasons. Yet these doctrinal reasons actually help us to understand the history of science. To begin with the last, since all human beings are made in the image God, and reason is our defining element, then it would make sense that all human beings—pagan, Islamic, Catholic, Protestant, and even atheist—could use their natural reason to inquire successfully into the order of nature. And that is what we find in the actual history of science: it is not solely a Christian activity. Nor is the Catholic Church at war with either science or reason. Since human reason is good, and human beings as such can understand by their own natural powers that God exists, and ever more deeply appreciate His wisdom manifest in creation (*Catechism*, paras. 27–49), then the activity of science is intrinsically good and licit for the Christian. That is why we find, all the way back to the early Middle Ages, a lively, sustained interest in philosophy and science (or as it was called, natural philosophy). We now turn to the Middle Ages to see just how important they were for the development of modern science.

THE SECOND CONFUSION

"The Middle Ages Were a Time of Scientific Darkness"

As we've noted, historians who assume that Christianity, and in particular Catholicism, is fundamentally antithetical to science have tended to neglect evidence from the Middle Ages to the contrary, leading to the rather absurd notion that quite suddenly modern science popped up out of nowhere. Thankfully, that old view has been discredited. Most historians now recognize that modern science did not begin in modernity; rather, it stands upon the shoulders of both ancient and medieval men.

Our task in this chapter, however, is not to provide a revised history of science that traces out all the details back to the ancient world but to use the deep history of science to understand the relationship of science to the Catholic Church. In particular, our purpose is to dispel the myth that throughout the Middle Ages, until around the 16th century, the Western world was shrouded in intellectual and scientific darkness. In order to do this most efficiently, we will focus on particular events, developments, themes, and figures that most tidily debunk this falsehood and, even more, illuminate the principles that define how the Catholic Church approaches science—those we've already mentioned and those we've yet to uncover.

Let's begin by going all the way back to ancient Babylon to uncover the oldest historical origins of modern science. Here, perhaps counterintuitively to the modern mind, we'll find the origins of modern science in ancient superstition. Here, too, we will discover the origin of the prevalent myth that the ancient Jews and their Bible were antiscientific, and that Christianity inherited the Jewish antipathy to science (hence the belief that scientific darkness reigned in medieval Christendom).

Astronomical Science in the Ancient World

Nearly every history of science today begins with the great, ancient Babylonian civilization, the land between the Tigris and Euphrates—interestingly enough, the land where the Bible begins, in Mesopotamia. The second creation account in the book of Genesis puts Adam and Eve in Eden, where there is a river that divides into four rivers: the Tigris, Euphrates, Pishon, and Gishon (Gen. 2:10–14). But we also hear about Babylon, with its infamous Tower of Babel—a temple structure called a ziggurat—which was the dwelling place of Babylon's city god. The idea behind building the ziggurat upward, platform by platform, was to point the temple toward the heavens, and so provide a connection between Earth and the gods.

It was on just such towers that science began.

There was a grand ziggurat at Ur, the splendid ancient Sumerian city from which Abram was called in the 19th century BC. Ur's ziggurat was dedicated to Nanna, the moon god (also known as Sin, his Akkadian name). Nanna was the greatest of the gods, and the creator. According to Babylonian religious mythology, he and his wife, the reed-goddess Ningal, brought forth offspring, Utu (the sun, his Akkadian name being Shamash) and Inanna (or Ishtar, the planet Venus, and goddess of fertility).[1]

But there is another profound connection between the ancient

Jews and Babylonians. In the sixth century BC, the Jews were taken from their beloved homeland and exiled among the Babylonians. In exile, they would have seen the seven-story ziggurat at Babylon, Etemenanki, "Temple of the Foundation of Heaven and Earth." The Babylonian creation myth, the *Enuma Elish*, has this ziggurat built just after the creation of the world. However that may be, it was most certainly in existence at the time of Abraham, and there was a restored version in the sixth century BC, built by the Babylonian King Nebuchadnezzar—the very king who conquered the Holy Land and dragged the Jews into exile. The ziggurat at Babylon was dedicated to Marduk, the supreme god, a position he achieved by defeating other gods.

Marduk was not the first of the gods. These were Apsu, the freshwater god, and Tiamet, the saltwater goddess, who gave birth to various deities who made such a ruckus that Apsu planned to destroy them—a plan thwarted by Tiamet, who brought Ea, the strongest of the offspring gods, to kill Apsu. Ea with his wife gave birth to Marduk, who himself caused trouble by stirring up winds that bothered Tiamet. Taking one of her sons, Kingu, as husband, Tiamet decided to gather the gods against Marduk, her grandson. Marduk slew Tiamet, forming the Earth from her corpse, and also killed Kingu, using his blood to make human beings. The gods, who had been enslaved by Marduk as punishment for warring against him, were relieved of their duties by the fashioning of human beings to be slaves to the gods.

One of Marduk's first tasks, undertaken before the making of man, was setting the heavens in order, positioning the gods as stars and planets, ordaining the year and having the moon god (Nanna) divide it into 12 months, and having the sun god (Shamash) divide it into days.

It is not difficult to see why the Babylonians would be interested in astrology—the sun, moon, planets, and stars were *deities*. And how wonderful an observatory tower a ziggurat makes for viewing the dance of the gods in the heavens! This great attention to the heavens was reinforced by the belief that there was a divinely mandated connection between what was going on in the heavens on what was happening on Earth. If something good happened on Earth, one could search the skies and find out what the positions of the heavenly bodies were; these positions, when they came around again, would mean a good omen. The same was true for bad things: one had only to see what positions the sun, moon, planets, and stars were in when they occurred to know in the future when the gods had evil in store for Earth once again.

That is the essence of astrology. Take note that it was not a private enterprise but one carried on by priests at the behest of the state. The Babylonian kings had a great interest in finding out what the heavens were saying in order to carry out their plans on Earth accordingly.

We find the first significant cataloguing of the heavens in Babylonia from about 1500 BC, and by then five planets were identified, each associated with a deity: as mentioned already, Venus with Inanna or Ishtar, Jupiter with Marduk, Saturn with Ninurta (an agricultural god), Mercury with Nabu (god of wisdom and writing), and Mars with Nergal (god of war, pestilence, and the dead).

Babylonian astronomy continued to develop even after the Babylonian Empire fell to the Persians in 539 BC, and the Greek Empire rose with Alexander the Great at the end of fourth century BC. The Babylonians' meticulously kept astrological records formed the foundation of modern astronomy, supplying the ancient Greeks with immensely detailed accounts of the rising and setting of the sun and moon and their positions in the sky, the exact positions of stars and planets over many, many years, and raw data about the occurrence of eclipses. The vast amount of data was necessary to begin the process of trying to sort out the regular motions of the heavenly bodies from the seemingly irregular ones, figure out a model of what the cosmos must be like, and successfully apply mathematics to it—a long, difficult

process culminating in the work of the great Greek astrono-
mer-astrologer Ptolemy in the second century AD. Without
the exhaustive astronomical-mathematical account in Ptolemy's
Almagest, Nicolaus Copernicus (1473–1543) would never have
had a picture detailed enough to spot the problems with it. Without Copernicus, there would have been no Galileo, and so on.

And What about the Ancient Jews?

And now look back over all this and note something very
curious. The Jews arose in a culture that practiced astrology in
Mesopotamia. During their spiritually intense formative period
in the Babylonian exile, they lived among the most highly developed astrologers of the ancient world. Two strange and related
facts here leap out at us.

First, in Genesis we find a creation story in which there is
only one God, and the sun, moon, and stars are merely lights.
When we compare the Genesis account to the Babylonian creation account, the *Enuma Elish*, Genesis seems intellectually and
religiously light-years ahead of the primitive Babylonian myth.
The difference is caused by the Jews' *rejection* of the common
notion—shared by ancient Babylonians, Egyptians, Canaanites,
and Greeks—that heavenly bodies were heavenly beings (as well
as the parallel notion that animals could be gods).

Second, *we find nothing astrological in the Old Testament*. The ancient
Jews seem not merely uninterested in it, but horrified by it, and
so Jewish Law specifically condemns divination (Lev. 19:26;
Deut. 18:9–11). That is why we don't find evidence in the Old
Testament for anything that looks like a precursor to modern
science. We instead find God saying to Abraham, "Look toward
heaven, and number the stars, if you are able to number them . . .
so shall your descendants be" (Gen. 15:5). The stars are not gods

controlling the fate of the people; they are lights that indicate the bounty of God's intended covenant blessing for His people.

There is more to this point. The Jews' belief that the world was set in order by one and only one God, that things in nature (in the heavens and on Earth) were natural and not divine, and that good crops, victory or defeat in battle, hail, rain, famine, pestilence, and plague came directly from God as *moral* rewards and punishments, kept the Jews from believing that the motions of the heavens determined their fortune. Their failure to hold the Promised Land was a moral failure, not the result of unhappy conjunctions of planets or constellations or the inability to calculate propitious ones.

And so, while the Babylonians were standing on their ziggurats, scanning the endless expanse of the heavens and detailing every motion of their divine denizens, the Jews, especially during the Babylonian exile, were turned within, scouring the spiritual and moral depths of their souls.

This had a decided effect on the Jews' consequent relationship to science. We do find significant interest in astronomy by Jews after the Babylonian exile (during what is called the Second Temple Period, 538 BC–AD 70), as well as during the period of classic rabbinic Judaism (AD 70–600), and on into the Middle Ages.[2] But we also find that they almost invariably approached astronomy as *subordinate* to biblical truths and interpretation.

For example, the *Book of Enoch* (1 Enoch) was written sometime during the third century BC. It describes Enoch (from Gen. 5:21–24) taken up into the heavens by the Angel Uriel, and shown the astronomical—not astrological—order of the heavens. In chapters 72–82, which scholars call the Astronomical Book, we find Enoch declaring, "The book of the courses of the luminaries of the heaven, the relations of each, according to their classes, their dominion and their seasons, according to their names and places of origin, and according to their months, which Uriel, the holy angel, who was with me, who is their guide, showed me; and he showed me all their laws exactly as they are, and how it is with regard to all the years of the world and unto eternity, till the new creation is accomplished which [en]dureth till eternity."[3]

Enoch is being shown the order of the heavens laid down by God. The sun, moon, planets, and stars obey God's laws—just as good Jews ought to do; they are not themselves divine, nor do they decide the fate of human affairs. As noted earlier in the *Book of Enoch*, in contrast to the orderly obedience of the heavens to God's commands, the bad Jews "have not been steadfast, nor done the commandments of the Lord/But . . . have turned away and spoken proud and hard words/With . . . impure mouths against His greatness" (1 Enoch 5:4). Along with this condemnation as contrast, the goal of the Astronomical Book is to make manifest the wonderful order of God's creation *and* to fix the Jewish calendar more accurately. Divination through astrology, by contrast, is presented as a wicked art taught by the wayward angels who mated with the women of Earth and produced the race of giants (Gen. 6:4; 1 Enoch 8:2). Even in later rabbinic literature, where the notion that the stars *do* determine human fate is taken seriously, the Jews are represented as an exception, removed from such determinism by God's special election.[4]

We have discovered an important principle governing the relationship of the Catholic Church to science, for the Catholic Church inherited the ancient Jewish abhorrence of astrological divination. To put it more broadly, the Church rejects all notions of science based on the belief that merely material forces (in the heavens or on Earth) are either divine, determine human actions, or both. St. Thomas Aquinas judiciously summed up the Church's position in his *Summa Theologiae*, where he tells us that divinization—the alleged astrological prediction of future contingent events—"is always a sin," a position that St. Thomas roots in both Deuteronomy and Church law.[5] Although physical forces may influence human choice, they do "not impose any necessity on the free-will, and man is able, by his reason, to act counter to the inclination of the heavenly bodies."

> Accordingly if anyone take observation of the stars in order to foreknow casual or fortuitous events, or to know with certitude future human actions, his conduct is based on a false and vain opinion; and so the operation of the demon introduces itself therein, wherefore it will be a superstitious and unlawful divination. On the other hand if one were to apply the observation of the stars in order to foreknow those future things that are caused by heavenly bodies, for instance, drought or rain and so forth, it will be neither unlawful nor a superstitious divination.[6]

For the Church, the theological and moral sciences must always remain the highest sciences because they deal with the highest, most comprehensive truths about God, the relationship of creation to God, and the moral life of human beings—the only creatures made in the image of God and capable of both good and evil. These are the primary truths revealed in the Bible. Compared to these truths, astronomical truths (however wonderful) are secondary. That having been said, astronomical truths, once shorn of astrology, are real truths; the heavens *do* declare the glory of God (Ps. 19).

Let's return to the ziggurat for one final point. The biblical account of the Tower of Babel presents the ziggurat as the great symbol of pride, "a tower with its top in the heavens" that allows the Babylonians to "make a name" for themselves (Gen. 11:1–9). The spirit of this effort to read the stars is illuminated in Isaiah (14:12–14), where the great prophet thunders against the Babylonian king, predicting his destruction, not by bad astrological omens, but the hand of the living God.

How you are fallen from heaven,
O Day Star, son of Dawn!
How you are cut down to the ground,
You who laid the nations low!
You said in your heart,
"I will ascend to heaven;
Above the stars of God
I will set my throne on high;
I will sit on the mount of assembly
In the far north;
I will ascend above the heights of the clouds,
I will make myself like the Most High."

The deepest, darkest temptation of astrology, and hence all bad science, is to believe that through the attainment of knowledge we become like God and so define good and evil and control our fates as if we were lords of the universe. In later Christian theology, the Day Star in this passage came to be associated with Lucifer. We have advanced far beyond Babylonian astrology in our science, but we are never beyond this temptation, and that is a truth more profound than any scientific truth.

The Dark and Middle Ages:
A Bridge between Ancient and Modern Science

As we've just seen, at least very briefly, the ancient origins of modern science go all the way back to the Babylonians, then through the Greeks. That was, of course, not the end of the story. Roman culture became the bearer of these ancient riches, and when the Roman Empire crumbled, first Islam and then Christianity took their turn.

If you trusted the propaganda of secularizing historians,

however, you would think that Christianity squandered those riches, broke the development of science, and that science was only struck up again in earnest in the late Renaissance. The truth is that Christianity was both the bearer of ancient science and an essential and significant contributor to it. This is nowhere clearer than in Christianity's greatest contribution to science, the invention of the university. "Put succinctly, the medieval period gave birth to the university, which developed with the active support of the papacy," points out historian of science Michael Shank.

> This unusual institution sprang up rather spontaneously around famous masters in towns like Bologna, Paris, and Oxford before 1200. By 1500, about sixty universities were scattered throughout Europe . . . About thirty percent of the medieval university curriculum covered subjects and texts concerned with the natural world. This was not a trivial development [for the history of science]. The proliferation of universities between 1200 and 1500 meant that hundreds of thousands of students—a quarter of a million in the German universities from 1350 on—were exposed to science in the Greco-Arabic tradition. As the universities mature, the curriculum came to include more works by [medieval] Latin masters who developed this tradition along original lines.
>
> If the medieval church had intended to discourage or suppress science, it certainly made a colossal mistake in tolerating—to say nothing of supporting—the university. In this new institution, Greco-Arabic science and medicine for the first time found a permanent home, one that—with various ups and downs—science has retained to this day.[7]

The medieval university—which was literally invented by Christendom—was also the conduit of ancient and early medieval

Islamic learning. It gave scholarship a definite structure in taking students through the seven liberal arts: the *quadrivium* (arithmetic, geometry, music, and astronomy) and *trivium* (grammar, rhetoric, and logic). Note the heavy emphasis on mathematics in the *quadrivium*—both music and astronomy are mathematically based. The mathematical foundation of modern science rests on the extraordinary spread of mathematical knowledge in the universities of Europe. It was, in fact, the cleric Adelard of Bath (c. 1080–1152) who translated Euclid's *Elements* into Latin, the single most influential mathematical treatise grounding early modern science. (Isaac Newton's *Philosophiae Naturalis Principia Mathematica* is heavily indebted to Euclid, as even a cursory examination of its structure attests.)

In the universities, even theology was taken up only after the intense study of the seven liberal arts. All theologians were first mathematicians and natural philosophers. Moreover, as the numbers provided by Shank attest, the universities of Christendom ensured that far more people were mathematically and scientifically literate than in any previous time. "Between 1150 and 1500," Shank notes, "more literate Europeans had had access to scientific materials than any of their predecessors in earlier cultures, thanks largely to the emergence, rapid growth, and naturalistic arts curricula of the medieval universities."[8] This disproves the idea that the Middle Ages were a time of scientific darkness.

Various and Sundry Other Myths

A lot of myths must be tossed out along with that one—for example, that medievals thought the Earth was flat and that it was only through the efforts of Christopher Columbus that its roundness was proven (against the protests of the monks). That the Earth was a sphere was well known in antiquity, attested by the pagans Aristotle, Eratosthenes, Ptolemy, Pliny the Elder,

Macrobius, and Christians such as St. Augustine, St. Jerome, St. Ambrose, and Boethius. Given that the medieval university was the conduit for both ancient astronomical learning and the thought of these great Saints, the notion that the medievals held obstinately to a flat Earth is ridiculous. The sphericity of the Earth was known by the "mathematical pope," Gerbert of Aurillac, crowned as Pope Sylvester II in 999.[9] It is attested by the 13th-century clerics St. Albert the Great, St. Thomas Aquinas, Michael Scot, and Roger Bacon. The most influential astronomical textbook used in the universities, written by the 13th-century cleric Jean de Sacrobosco, was *De Sphera*, obviously not a work touting a flat Earth. Another popular work, *Imago Mundi* (1410)—so popular, it was read by none other than Christopher Columbus—also argued for the sphericity of the Earth. It was written by Pierre d'Ailly, the archbishop of Cambrai.[10] They even knew the approximate size of the circumference of the Earth, setting it at 29,000 miles[11] (the actual size being about 24,900 miles at the equator).

We must also let go of the notion that medieval philosophers thought that the universe was a very small sphere surrounding a very large Earth. We get this notion from representations of the cosmos, made during the Middle Ages, that (like other art during the period) doesn't put things in proper perspective. These illustrations invariably try to squeeze everything into one picture, and so show a relatively large Earth at the center with the rest of the cosmos, including the outer heavens, surrounding it and taking up about the same size as the Earth. But that isn't how educated medieval men viewed the size of the Earth; in fact, it was quite the contrary, as the great early sixth-century Christian philosopher and theologian Boethius makes clear. "It is well known and you have seen it demonstrated by astronomers," Boethius remarks, in his famous *Consolation of Philosophy*, "that beside the extent of the heavens, the circumference of the Earth has the size of a point; that is to say, compared to the magnitude of the celestial sphere, it may be thought of as having no extent at all."[12]

And how big did they think the "celestial sphere" surrounding Earth was? Calculations by Arab astronomers, which were passed on to the Middle Ages, put the distance from the Earth to the stars at about 90,000,000 miles.[13] In the popular 14th-century hagiographical work, the *South England Legendary*, we are told that a man could not reach the highest Heaven if he were to travel 40 miles a day for 8,000 years, that is, for over 116,800,000 miles.[14]

Of course, the medievals did deny that the Earth moved, and they did affirm that the Earth, insignificant as it was, was the center of the universe. Yet, when we look at their reasoning, we don't find stupidity, obscurantism, or pride, but logic and humility. Pope Sylvester II was, again, both a mathematician and astronomer. He knew that given the size of the Earth (which, again, he got about right), if it rotated every 24 hours he would be traveling at about 1,000 miles per hour on the surface. If that were so, he and others reasoned, then he should be blown over by the wind and objects thrown into the air would land far behind him.[15] There were no rational arguments at the time against such rational objections.

And how should we account for the idea of the Earth being the center of the universe? As we shall see in more detail in the next chapter, that was not a matter of theological pride. The medieval believed, based on Aristotle, that up was better, and as one moved away from the Earth, one was moving up toward Heaven, toward the ethereal, blissful, and imperishable. Earth was at the center of the universe because it was the lowest point, in every sense of the term: it was of insignificant size, and it was a kind of sinkhole where all that was heavy, ephemeral, and corruptible gathered. The only thing lower, more in the center, in fact at the center of the Earth, was Hell.[16]

A Host of Medieval Scientists

If you read any recent history of science, one that attends to the actual facts, you'll find that the list of scientists from the Middle Ages is almost exclusively a list of priests, religious brothers, bishops, and cardinals. A lay scientist was as rare as a hen's tooth until the 16th and 17th centuries, and even then, Catholic clerics (as well as laymen) continued to make up a large percentage of those moving science forward. Without these medieval men of God, there would have been no modern science. Without this historical cause, the history of science would have died with the ancients.

The signal importance of this position, of being the bearer and developer of science, during the period running from about AD 1100 to 1500, must be understood. Human beings are not instant knowers, and so they are not instant scientists. The road to discovery is slow and long, and every part of that road is necessary for every part that succeeds it. Modern science depends essentially on the bearing forward and developing of astronomy, mathematics, geometry, logic, alchemy, optics, and so on, carried out during the Middle Ages by churchmen. Although some of the work they did may sound primitive today, that is only because we depend historically and intellectually on their achievements even—and especially—for our ability to surpass them. All later parts of the history of science depend on the earlier, and that is why any history of science today includes the following figures.

- The Dominican friar Albertus Magnus, or St. Albert the Great (c. 1193–1280), is the patron saint of the sciences, earning his title by being one of the most outspoken defenders of a churchman's right to explore the natural world. St. Albert gathered together all the best about natural philosophy, astronomy, physiology, mineralogy, alchemy, biology, botany, as well as ethics, politics, mathematics, metaphysics, and theology, and tried to bring order to it all. Bringing order out of disorder, in regard to previous research, is an essential step for the advance of science. But we should not miss the theological point St. Albert was making: the study of nature and the study of God go hand in hand, for God's glory, love, and wisdom are shown in His works of creation and in His work of redemption.

- Robert Grosseteste (c. 1170–1253), the bishop of Lincoln, was both a zealous reformer of the Church and a zealous scientist, one of the leading mathematicians and natural philosophers of his time. He wrote a textbook on astronomy and the structure of the world, and works on light, the movement of tides, mathematics, comets, and the rainbow.

- Roger Bacon (c. 1214–94), a Franciscan friar, emphasized (with the ancient philosopher, Aristotle) that experience—*experimentum*—was essential to progress in science and gathered together and attempted to synthesize the available theories on light and optics. He also speculated on the possibility of creating vehicles that moved without horses, on flying machines, and much more within his realm of possibility, a looking glass that would make very distant objects appear much closer.

- The Franciscan archbishop of Canterbury John Peckham (c. 1230–92) and his contemporary Erasmus Witelo, a Polish friar, also advanced optical theory, writing treatises that formed the foundation of the university curriculum and hence the foundation of the advances of modern optics. (And, by the way, reading spectacles were invented sometime in the late 13th century.) The Benedictine Richard of Wallingford (1292–1336), the son of a blacksmith, was the abbot of St. Albans and invented the Albion: an astronomical instrument that very cleverly allowed its user to determine the position of the stars and planets without cumbersome (and sometimes, not very accurately copied) astronomical tables. Even more, being a keen craftsman and a fine mathematician enabled him to build a masterful mechanical clock, the best of its day, for the abbey church. (Ingeniously, its face was an astrolabe.) Clocks not only were interesting in their own right but were initially built for a very theological purpose: to help the monks structure their days of prayer and work, *ora et labora*.[17] It would, of course, be rather difficult to carry out the precise measurements of speed in modern science without ever more precise measurements of time. Then there were the so-called Merton Calculators of Oxford's Merton College, such as Thomas Bradwardine (c. 1290–1349), who stressed the importance for using mathematics in the natural sciences and attempted to derive a formula of motion. There was also Richard Swineshead, known as The Calculator because of his extraordinary mathematical abilities, who flourished in the mid-14th century. Swineshead's *Liber calculationum, Book of Calculations*, was the premier, cutting-edge mathematics book of the day. And then we have William Heytesbury (c. 1313–73), who correctly formulated a mean speed theorem that dealt with calculations of distance covered over a period of time under uniform acceleration—again, an important landmark in the history of physics. The German Dominican Theodoric of Freiburg (c. 1250–1310) gave the world the first correct geometrical analysis of the rainbow—a triumph of the union of optics, geometry, and natural philosophy.

- The Frenchman and cleric John Buridan (c. 1300–1361) formulated the basics of modern impetus theory used in predicted projectile motion and in astronomy, for the continual motion of the stars and planets. He also gave one of the original, rational replies to the problems entailed in suggesting that the Earth itself might be rotating (rather than the heavens rotating around the Earth). As we've mentioned, previously the rational response to someone suggesting that we were spinning at a thousand miles an hour was "Why don't we feel or see the obvious effects of this motion?" Buridan offered the right solution: the air, or atmosphere, surrounding the Earth might be rotating with it. Buridan's student, who became the bishop of Lisieux, Nicole Oresme (c. 1323–82) refined his master's solution to the motion problem, as well as William Heytesbury's mean speed theorem.

The "Light Ages"

We must stress the obvious connections between the universities, the universal Church, and the work of the clerical scientists we've briefly mentioned. The universities of Christendom provided the teaching context that allowed significant achievements to be made (since the liberal arts curriculum demanded of all students a knowledge of both mathematics and natural philosophy), promoted the advancement of each of the sciences, and perhaps most important of all, provided a universal language and geographically fluid culture that allowed students and scholars all over Europe to communicate and collaborate with each other. And we cannot neglect to mention again the sheer *numbers* of people in the universities; since the religious orders, especially the mendicant orders, were open to every level of society, this represented the largest expanse of scientific knowledge in the history of the world up to that point.

So, far from being a dark time for science, during the Middle Ages light was being shed like never before. But that doesn't mean that there were not dark spots, and the darkest occurred in the mid-14th century with the Black Death. We cannot overestimate the horrifying effects of having perhaps half of the European population wiped out by an unknown, and at the time unknowable, contagion. The Black Death took anyone and everyone, from noble to peasant, scholar to serf, and the intellectual and scientific culture that had been built up in the university system from the 11th to the 14th century suffered a very severe blow. This devastating setback explains the chaos and confusion found in the mid-14th century and for decades thereafter. Science, in a very real sense, is a luxury of civilization; when civilization itself is threatened at its moorings, luxuries give way to dealing with necessities.

The thread of scientific progress would pick up again with still another cleric, one Nicolaus Copernicus, but our consideration of him is best left for the next chapter.

The Third Confusion

"The Anti-science Catholic Church Persecuted Copernicus and Galileo"

If you listened to the rumors that have passed for history, you would think that the truth about Copernicus and Galileo was something like this. Before Copernicus, science was in the dark thrall of ignorant monks and corrupt churchmen. Quite suddenly one day, a man named Copernicus dared to point out that the Earth was not flat but round and that the sun was still and the Earth revolved around it. For his noble efforts, he was immediately burned to death on an already smoldering pile of heretics.

Soon after that, though, came an Italian physicist named Galileo Galilei, who looked through his telescope and saw quite clearly that the sun was still and the Earth moved and fearlessly spoke out in favor of the truth. For his noble efforts, the Church threw him in jail, tortured him mercilessly for years, and on several special Church holidays hung him at dawn, drew and quartered him at noon, and burned him on the stake in the evenings (using all his books for fuel).

Of course, this montage of absurd episodes is without historical foundation. As we'll see, neither Copernicus nor Galileo ever went to jail, although Galileo spent some time under very comfortable "house arrest." Neither were tortured or burned or executed in any other way. Both died in their own beds:

Copernicus from the effects of a stroke and Galileo of other natural causes.

Yet, the old myths do not die easily, and even among the most eminent scientists of our own day, who should certainly know better, rumors pass for truths. Our most famous theoretical physicist, Stephen Hawking, though he likely knows Galileo wasn't tortured or burned, still had this to say: "Galileo's renowned conflict with the Catholic Church was central to his philosophy. He was one of the first to argue that human beings could hope to understand how the world works, and, moreover, that we could do this by observing the real world. Galileo, perhaps more than any other single person, was responsible for the birth of modern science."[1]

Galileo was certainly not "one of the first to argue that human beings could hope to understand how the world works . . . by observing the real world." If any one man could be given such credit, it would be the ancient Greek philosopher Aristotle. But as we've seen, the Church's emphasis on knowing God *through* nature grounded the entire medieval preoccupation with science, in particular, astronomy. Hawking is entirely misrepresenting the significance of Galileo and simply rewarming a version of Draper and White's warfare myth.

Obviously, Hawking has not done much reading in the history of science, or he would have known better. Let's see what the record looks like when it's been set straight.

The Great Copernican Cliché

Let's begin with the significance of what Copernicus did. Nicolaus Copernicus was born in February of 1473 in the city of Toruń, in northern Poland. His parents were part of the merchant class, and must have been devout, as two of his three siblings entered religious life. Nicolaus was extremely well educated, speaking five languages, and was a gifted beneficiary of the mathematical-astronomical heritage of the university systems. It was at the University of Krakow that he learned the Ptolemaic system thoroughly. He may have become a priest, or he may only have taken minor orders, but in either case, he was a man of the Church and earned a doctorate in Canon Law. He also studied medicine at the University of Padua. After these studies, Copernicus moved back to Poland, and it is there that he lived out his life working on his great astronomical alternative to Ptolemy. By 1514 he had sketched out some aspects of his theory and by the early 1530s he had more or less completed his famous *De revolutionibus orbium coelestium* (*On the revolution of the heavenly spheres*) but held off having it published until he was on his deathbed in 1543.

What to make of his "revolution"? As nearly everyone knows, Copernicus argued for a heliocentric (sun-centered) astronomical system against a geocentric (Earth-centered) astronomical system. The significance of this has been popularly touted as a great reality check for humanity—a demotion from our self-appointed (and Bible-supported) high pedestal in the universe. By the Copernican revolution, so the story goes, man was torn from his exalted position at the center of creation and cast outward as a humbled denizen of one among several other planets orbiting the sun. Science triumphantly dethroned man and theology both! (Sound familiar? It's part of the warfare thesis.)

So goes the "great Copernican cliché," which, as Dennis Danielson remarks, "for a good number of years, even centuries, has been cluttering up our understanding of the history of astronomy, and of history generally," and "which has been repeated so often, and by such respectable voices, that it is now virtually a part of everyone's mental furniture. That, of course, is the nature of a cliché: It is a statement whose very frequency of repetition results, independent of its truth or falsehood, in its being repeated yet again."[2] As Danielson shows, the cliché is as false as it is influential by repetition.

One part of the cliché supposes that the conflict between the heliocentric and geocentric views is essentially a conflict between science and theology, as if the *only* reason that one would believe that the Earth was the stationary center of the universe is that it was mandated by faith (and sternly enforced by Church authorities). But that is manifestly false. The ultimate authority was the very real, commonsense experience of standing on a still Earth and looking up at the sky and observing that the sun, moon, stars, and planets reel around us. Whatever the Church and the Bible had to say rested on this seemingly quite solid foundation of commonsense experience.

Moreover, it was on this commonsense assumption that all astronomy had hitherto been built. In the second century, Ptolemy brought together all the best astronomical observations of the ancient world and united them in a systematic account, which in turn became the foundation on which Islamic and medieval Christian astronomers would build. As with all well-developed scientific paradigms, it could not (and should not) easily be let go without extraordinary evidence and argument to the contrary.

When he set down his new system, then, Copernicus's main adversary was not, in fact, the Church but the status quo of *science*. Contrary to the cliché, there were no recognizable advantages for adopting Copernicus's system when his now famous *De Revolutionibus* was published in 1543 and little had changed by the time of Galileo a generation later. In fact, the greatest astronomer of the time, Tycho Brahe (1546–1601), had proposed a variation on the Ptolemaic system (wherein the Earth retained its central position, the sun still revolving around it, but five of the planets revolved around the sun). Brahe's new and detailed observations of the stars and planets were, arguably, the single most important advance making modern astronomy possible because his acute eye—the telescope wasn't invented quite yet—gave Europeans the greatly improved astronomical tables without which no real argument about the heavens, one way or another, could effectively take place.

It is often maintained, as part of the Copernican cliché, that Ptolemy's system was muddled with the endless rigging of circles and epicycles (circles spinning on circles) to make it fit the way the planets actually appeared to move and that Copernicus offered a simpler, more "economical" alternative without all the ad hoc geometrical apparatus. The truth is otherwise. Copernicus's *De revolutionibus* was in fact so mathematically difficult that only very few people of the time could penetrate it.

As historian of science Thomas Kuhn put it, the alleged "economy of the Copernican system . . . is largely an illusion." The seven-circle system set out by Copernicus in the first book of the *De revolutionibus* "will not predict the position of planets with an accuracy comparable to that supplied by Ptolemy's [12-circle] system." Ptolemy had indeed "been compelled to complicate the fundamental 12-circle system with minor epicycles, eccentrics, and equants," but "to get comparable results from his basic seven-circle system Copernicus, too, was forced to use minor epicycles and eccentrics." Kuhn concludes, "His [Copernicus's] full system was little if any less cumbersome than Ptolemy's had been. Both employed over 30 circles; there was little to choose between them in economy. Nor could the two systems be distinguished by their accuracy. When Copernicus had finished adding circles, his cumbersome sun-centered system gave results as accurate as Ptolemy's but it did not give more accurate results. Copernicus did not solve the problem of the planets."[3] That is, of course, not to say that Copernicus's system was ultimately no better than Ptolemy's. But *at the time* it could not have been known to be superior, based on Copernicus's own most famous work. Thus, resistance to the Copernican system was fully justified at the time *on scientific grounds alone*, and that is why the main resistance to it came from other astronomers. In opposing Copernicus, then, the Church did not act unscientifically, but in fact relied on the authority and competence of the best astronomers of the day.

Another aspect of the Copernican cliché says that holding to

Earth-centeredness was a matter of theological pride, of the belief, taken from the Bible, that our central place in the plan of redemption means that Earth must be located the center of the universe. But that is sheer invention.

In Aristotle's cosmological understanding, which grounded the Ptolemaic view, there were four elements: Earth, water, air, and fire, in an ascending scale from heavy to light, and more important, base to noble, earthly to heavenly. Throw some dirt up in the air. What happens? It falls down. Dirt is dirty, heavy, gross. In the Aristotelians' view, that's why the Earth was at the center—not because it was exalted but because it was the most ignoble place. In Danielson's words,

> Pre-Copernican cosmology pointed not to the metaphysical or axiological "centrality" but rather to the sheer grossness of humankind and its abode. In this view, the Earth appears as a universal pit, figuratively as well as literally the world's low point. As C. S. Lewis puts it, the medieval model is in fact not anthropocentric but "anthropoperipheral." This negative view encompasses, finally, not only ancient and medieval Arabic, Jewish, and Christian writers, but also many prominent voices that we usually associate with Renaissance humanism, both before and after the time of Copernicus. Giovanni Pico (1463–1494), even within a work that acquired the title *Oration on the Dignity of Man* (1486), refers to our present dwelling place the Earth as "the excrementary and filthy parts of the lower world." And a quarter century after the publication of *De revolutionibus*, in 1568, Michel de Montaigne takes up the same theme once more, declaring that we are "lodged here in the dirt and filth of the world, nailed and rivetted to the worst and deadest part of the universe, in the lowest story of the house, and most remote from the heavenly arch."[4]

This low opinion of the Earth was, of course, in place at the time of Galileo as well, and so Galileo himself could use it on behalf of Copernicanism, arguing that it lifts Earth up to participate in the "dancing whirl of stars," rather than (with Ptolemaic astronomy) allowing the Earth to be "the sink of all dull refuse of the universe."[5] Lifting it out of the sink was, for Galileo, a way of exalting the Earth. As Danielson says, "In Ptolemaic cosmology, the place of Earth is both low and lowly. But in contrast, the cosmology of Copernicus and Galileo is, in more senses than one, *uppity*"[6]—the *exact opposite of the cliché*.

What would be the cause of the cliché's turning the truth upside down? We do not have far to look, according to Danielson: the secularist notion that science is at war with religion and the forces of light against the forces of darkness. As Danielson maintains, "the great Copernican cliché is in some respects more than just an innocent confusion."

> Rather, it functions as a self-congratulatory story that materialist modernism recites to itself as a means of displacing its own hubris onto what it likes to call the "Dark Ages."
> But the trick of this supposed dethronement is that, while purportedly rendering "Man" less cosmically and metaphysically important, it actually enthrones us modern "scientific" humans in all our enlightened superiority. It declares, in effect, *"We're truly very special because we've shown that we're not so special."*[7]

In other words, as a kind of revolutionary force, secularism has a vested interest in the notion that with the Church, pride and stupidity were ceremoniously wedded. In truth, before the new paradigm offered by Copernicus could be accepted, it had to demonstrate its scientific superiority to the Ptolemaic system (which its proponents began to do only in the 17th century), and it had to overcome the significant philosophical and common-sense objections lodged against it.

And finally, the theological objections, based in Scripture, also had to be dealt with. Again, though, we must insist on the obvious: the reason the Earth is described as stationary in the Bible is precisely because it *is* stationary, for us, as a matter of experience. What sense would the Bible have made to anyone if it *began* with the counterintuitive notion that the Earth was both spinning on its own axis and circling the sun at alarming speeds without any of the dense, advanced scientific explanation, based on advanced mathematics and astronomical observations unavailable to the human race until after many centuries of arduous intellectual development?

It is true, however, to point out that for some, the scriptural foundation was first and foremost, and that is perhaps why, among Christians, Protestants were the first to lodge Bible-based objections to Copernicanism. But even here, we find the assumption that the science of astronomy itself also spoke against heliocentricism. In 1539, even before Copernicus's work was published, Martin Luther caught wind of it and said of Copernicus, "This fool wishes to reverse the entire science of astronomy," before adding also that "sacred Scripture tells us that Joshua commanded the sun to stand still, and not the Earth." Other Protestants leaned on Scripture alone. In 1549, Luther's follower Melanchthon stated, against Copernicus's "love of novelty," that "it is part of a good mind to accept the truth as revealed by God and to acquiesce in it." Citing the 93rd Psalm, that "the world is established; it shall never be moved," John Calvin, in his *Commentary on Genesis*, then asked, "Who will venture to place the authority of Copernicus above that of the Holy Spirit?"[8]

But the Catholic Church also put its foot down. In March of 1616—over 70 years after the publication of Copernicus's *De revolutionibus*—the Church's Congregation of the Index of Forbidden Books officially stated that to assert that the Earth rotated around the sun was scientifically "foolish and absurd," *and also* it was contrary to Scripture.[9] The Church did not ban Copernicus's work but suspended its publication until it could be corrected. They were quite willing to allow it as a mathematical means or method that might yield easier calculations of planetary orbits, as long as it did not assert heliocentricism to be true.

This might seem to us to be an absurd position, but it was based on the quite reasonable principle—enunciated first by Aristotle, elaborated more fully by St. Thomas Aquinas,[10] and still true today—that mathematical constructs do not, in and of themselves, tell you about the *nature* or *reality* of the things they describe. (That's why multiple equations in science can describe the same phenomena, or mathematical data can be interpreted in various, even contradictory ways by different scientists.) In astronomy, the mathematical and geometrical apparatus simply allows you to tell *where* planets or stars are going to be at a particular time, not *what* they are made of, *how* and *why* they travel the paths they do, or even more mysteriously, how and why the very human science of mathematics is so wonderfully applicable to the motions in the heavens. For this reason, astronomy was known as an "intermediate science" among the medievals, a science that used mathematics to describe physical motion, without offering a theoretical account of either mathematics or physical motion. Given the intellectual tradition of understanding mathematics as applied to the motions of the heavens in this way, the Church's acceptance of Copernicus's system as merely a mathematical construct handy for calculations makes complete sense. That's how it understood all mathematically based astronomy.

A month before the official prohibition of teaching or defending the proposition that the sun was the center of the universe, the Church had warned the famous astronomer Galileo "to abandon completely the above-mentioned opinion that the sun stands still at the center of the world and the Earth moves, and henceforth not to hold, teach, or defend it in any way whatever, either orally or in writing; otherwise the Holy Office would start proceedings against him."[11] In 1620, the Congregation released its corrected version of Copernicus's *De revolutionibus* with a mere handful of amendments, enough to reduce it from a statement about reality to a mathematical hypothesis.[12] One could *assume* that the Earth moved around the sun for purposes of calculation but not *assert* that it actually moved.

Galileo was not satisfied, and to Galileo we now turn.

What about Galileo?

As with Copernicus, our goal is to disengage the Galileo affair from the misinformation that has arisen, in great part from the warfare myth. As we've already become well aware, the Catholic Church did not object to science, but was in fact its main patron right up to, and through, the time of Galileo, and of course, down to the present day. So we must clear away the myths and draw together the rather complex facts.

Galileo Galilei was also born in Pisa, Italy in 1564. He was the son of a famous musician and the first of six children. As his early studies revealed, he was an obviously gifted mathematician, and Galileo was appointed to teach as a chair of mathematics in Pisa by 1589 and soon moved on to the University of Padua. In 1610, Galileo achieved Europe-wide fame with the publication of his discovery of the moons of Jupiter through his improved version of the telescope, and part of this presentation revealed his advocacy of Copernicanism. Six years later he was warned, officially, by one Cardinal Bellarmino, not to advocate or teach Copernicanism.

In 1623 Galileo published *The Assayer*, a treatise that quite openly seemed to advocate a kind of Democritan atomism, that is, an ancient materialist doctrine also associated with the pagan atheism of Epicurus and Lucretius. In that same year, one of Galileo's friends and admirers, Cardinal Maffeo Barberini, was elected Pope Urban VIII, and Galileo was emboldened to speak out, if even circumspectly, on behalf of Copernicanism. The result was his *Dialogue Concerning Two Chief World Systems* (1632), which rather cleverly but disingenuously argued for the superiority of the Copernican view, though not its absolute truth.

Galileo was summoned to Rome for trial the following year and found guilty of a particular grade of heresy—not the most serious, but not trivial either. The sentencing document included a note that during the interrogation "we deemed it necessary to proceed against you by a rigorous examination," and "We condemn you to formal imprisonment in this Holy Office at our pleasures."[13] The first might lead to the conclusion that Galileo was actually tortured, and the second, quite obviously, that he was imprisoned. Both were plausible inferences for quite a long time, until other evidence arose.

The notion that Galileo was actually tortured has now been shown to be false, although he was threatened with torture. As for imprisonment, while Galileo may have been in a prison for about three days (although it is more likely he stayed in the prosecutor's apartment), he actually spent his time during the trial and afterward in secluded luxury, first at the Tuscan embassy, then at the Inquisition palace in the six-room apartment of the prosecutor himself (complete with a servant), then later at the luxurious palace of the Medici in Rome; after this, he was under house arrest at his friend the archbishop's residence in Siena, and then finally, in his own house at Arcetri, near Florence, where he stayed from 1633 to his death in 1642, a frail man of 77.[14]

All that having been said, we still might shudder at the thought that Galileo was arrested at all, that he was even remotely threatened with torture, and that he remained under arrest if even in his own house. How could this have happened and why? To understand, we must take a look at the much larger historical context, beginning with philosophy.

Here especially we will learn a lesson about why, when studying the history of science, one cannot study just the history of science. As noted earlier, in 1623 Galileo had published a book, *The Assayer*, in which he advocated quite openly the materialist position of the ancient pagan philosopher Democritus (c. 460–370 BC) against the Aristotelianism of his day. In perfect accord with Democritus, Galileo asserted that "whenever I conceive any material or corporeal substance, I immediately think of it as bounded, and as having this or that shape," but

> that it must [also] be white or red, bitter or sweet, noisy or silent, and of sweet or foul odor, my mind does not feel compelled to bring in as necessary accompaniments . . . Hence I think that tastes, odors, colors, and so on are no more than mere names so far as the object in which we place them is concerned, and that they reside only in the consciousness. Hence if the living creature were removed, all these qualities would be wiped away and annihilated. But since we have imposed upon them special names, distinct from those of the other and real qualities [of shape] mentioned previously, we wish to believe that they really exist as actually different from those.[15]

It is difficult for us, having accepted the basic tenets of modern materialism, to see materialist atomism as alarming or strange at its inception. But this we must do, or we will not understand the alarm at the time.

Democritus asserted that there were only two realities in the universe: eternal, indestructible atoms and the void. Everything else was made up of these two things, and only these two things. Thus, everything we experience with our senses—that things have color, that they have smell, that they have odor, that they are hot or cold, and so on—are illusory. Or more exactly, the shapes, sizes, and motion of invisible material atoms cause, in us, particular sensations that we (falsely) believe reveal something real about the thing we are sensing. The apple isn't *really* red; red-ness is what we call the sensation in us of color that is caused by the shape of the atoms hitting the atoms of our material body. Redness has no reality; it is a mere name.

Even stranger, the apple really isn't an apple. All sensible things, from apples to oranges, trees to flowers, dogs to cats, are just agglomerations of atoms. The shapes they happen to have and the way they happen to act are entirely reducible to their atomic structure. The atoms are real; their subsensible microscopic shapes are real; but the shape of the agglomeration we can see, feel, and touch is a mere accident of all the atomic parts having been put together in a certain way. Like a boy's dinosaur made out of Lego building blocks or a sand sculpture of a whale, the apple itself isn't real but entirely reducible to its constituent parts, atoms. Therefore, the words "apple," "orange," "tree," "flower," "dog," "cat" are, like "red," merely names we give to the differ-ent, unique collections of atoms.

Mere names—that should remind us of that persistent philo-sophical aberration of the Middle Ages, nominalism, associated with William of Ockham (c. 1288–1348). Ockham, too, was an atomist, and insisted that our names for things had no connec-tion to reality and so were mere names (nominalism coming from the Latin *nomen*, "name"). Our grouping of things by name, both on the most general level and on the more specific—cats, dogs, trees; Siamese, Beagle, oak—was a mere convenience because we make our judgments based on mere surface similarity. In reality, all things are purely individual—a theory that makes sense if you believe that what is real is the individual collections of atoms.

In denying that names had any real connection to things as we experience them—we do not experience things as agglomerations of subsensible atoms—Ockham destroyed the commonsense connection between our speech and being, between word and creation. That had natural and (although Ockham did not intend it) supernatural implications. Nominalism severs the natural connection between the way we normally think and speak and the way the world really *is*, and in doing so, removes (among other things) the real connection between the revelation through words in the Bible and the truth of what God is trying to reveal. Since God's wisdom is made evident through His creation, and the Jews, as with everyone else, believed that their words were connected to real things in creation, nominalism makes hash of our connection to God's wisdom through our ordinary natural reason. But even more, since Jesus Christ is understood to be the Word through Whom all things were made, the Word Himself made flesh and the fulfillment of the words of Holy Scripture, nominalism overturns the rich theology based on the natural-supernatural connections between God's Word, the things of the world made through His Word, and our words. How can grace build on nature when nature as we experience it has no real connection to the atomic reality that actually defines nature?

In combating both atomism and nominalism, the Church had sided with Aristotle, the ancient Greek philosopher of common sense, who insisted that the names we use *do* correspond to the real forms of things, so that (for example) *this cat* is a unity of form (what makes it a living *cat*, uniting its matter in a complex, living being that is a member of a particular species) and matter (what makes it *this* particular cat). It is of no small interest to note that both Ockham in the 14th century and Galileo in the 17th century were using atomism to overturn Aristotle.

But why were they doing this? For Ockham, the influence of the pagan Aristotle threatened to eclipse the authority of revelation. So he thought he must ruin Aristotle for the sake of faith, even if he ruined common sense along with it (and, ironically, faith too). For Galileo, Aristotle represented all that was old and unenlightened, and more particularly, the main obstacle to producing a new physics based on atomism, which he thought to be the most promising approach to natural philosophy. But whatever their motives, we must understand this to understand the

Galileo affair: when Galileo embraced atomism and nominalism in *The Assayer*, the Church saw him as a bearer of old philosophical errors with which they were all too familiar. Moreover, the overturning of common sense that occurs with atomism and nominalism alarmed the Church even more than the overturning of common sense that was entailed in Copernicanism.

But there are further implications of atomism, which were brought out very clearly by the Greek pagan philosopher Epicurus (341–270 BC) and his first-century-BC Roman disciple Lucretius. If atoms and the void are the only reality, then there are no such things as immaterial souls. We human beings are mere agglomerations of atoms, an accident of their material substance.

For Epicurus, that is a great boon, as he considered religion and the fear of punishment in Hades by the gods to be the chief source of human anxiety. His materialism eliminated both religion and fear of the gods' punishment, for at death, since we are only material bodies, our atoms disassociate and we exist no longer. Furthermore, as the hedonistic sense attached today to the word "Epicurean" hints, since there were no souls, the moral domain of good and evil had to be transferred entirely to the body. Epicurus therefore identified the good with the physically pleasurable (even though he himself was ascetic) and evil with what is physically painful, thus ultimately yielding an ethics where the pursuit of pleasure defines what is good and the avoidance of pain what is evil.

Lucretius furthered the development of Epicurean materialism, packaging it in his great Latin poem "De Rerum Natura," which argues elegantly for the entire materialist atomistic theory, including its antireligious bent, and adds a theory of generation of all living things by the random association of material atomic particles—a Darwinian-type evolutionary theory about 2,000 years before Darwin. As with Epicurus, the goal was to remove the need for God the Creator.[16]

We must emphasize the obvious: Christians were, from the

very first, entirely antagonistic to the materialist doctrines of Democritan atomism precisely because they were so intimately associated with the atheism and hedonism of the Epicureans. Thus during Christianity's first four centuries we observe a storm of holy invective showered upon the names of Epicurus and his disciple Lucretius by such Christian luminaries as St. Athanasius, St. Gregory of Nyssa, St. Basil, St. Ambrose, and most influential of all, St. Augustine. This animus became the foundation for the Catholic suspicion of any attempt to base a physics on material atoms, and it was firmly in place in the early Renaissance when the ancient works of or about Epicurus and Lucretius were recovered and began to circulate around Europe. The predictable effect of this widespread circulation was a new interest in atomism—especially as defined against the natural philosophy of Aristotle—and even more important, a revival of atheism and hedonism. All of this happened in the time period leading right up to Galileo.[17]

And, we must add, when Epicurean atomism saturated European philosophical thought, and thanks to men like Descartes, Locke, and Hobbes became firmly imbedded as the foundation of the new materialism, *it did in fact* bring about the secularization of society that Epicurus intended and the Church feared. Predictably, once all bodies, including our bodies, were considered to be macroscopic effects of microscopic material causes, the soul became a problem. If the body worked as a kind of atomically driven mechanism, what need had we for a soul? We live in a mostly secularized world today largely because we've accepted such materialism as true, and so we, agreeing with Epicurus, no longer believe in immaterial souls but rather take even our bodily reality to be merely the effect of our subsensible chemical structure.

Now, none of this is offered so that we might conclude that Galileo should have been jailed, tortured, or killed! The point, rather, is this: it is completely understandable that the assertion of Democritan atomism by Galileo would set off serious alarms among philosophers and theologians of the 17th century. They were, by intellectual training, rightly habituated to associate such atomism with the atheism and hedonism of Epicurus and Lucretius.

I say "habituated" to make us aware that there was at least the possibility that Democritan atomism might be reconceived so that it could fit with a Christian understanding of the world. In fact, men such as the Catholic priest Pierre Gassendi and the pious Protestant Robert Boyle attempted just that. But there is no doubt, from reading their defenses of Christianized atomism, that they lived in a culture in which atomism was so heavily suspected of irreligion that they had to publicly disavow the connection and show at great length how Christianity and materialist atomism could be reconciled. And there is no doubt that they lived in a time in which the recovery and spread of materialist atomism had indeed brought men to embrace atheism.

Now here I offer an interesting conjecture, one that I think is well founded. If Galileo had *only* avowed Copernicanism (and done so with a little more humility and tact), he might have avoided any trouble at all. But the combination of the two—atomism and Copernicanism—tended to make his Copernicanism smell of Epicureanism. Why? What possible connection could there be between the two?

Again, Epicurus's goal was to destroy any notion that we had an immortal soul that could be bothered in the afterlife by the gods. Materialism allowed him to be entirely this-worldly and live his brief life on Earth in peace and without worry. The notion that the random association of atoms brings about *everything* we know, including ourselves, was a double assurance that there is no creator who has any claims upon us.

But there was even more to the Epicurean cosmology that made it god-proof: Epicurus's assertion of an infinite universe, infinite time, and a multiplicity of worlds. To make it plausible that mere random association of atoms could create our world, Epicurus argued that in fact the Earth was not special at all, because the random association of infinite atoms jostling for infinite time created a plurality of worlds, countless numbers of which were peopled by intelligent creatures. If our world was created by the random association of atoms, and we are just one of innumerable planets (and most likely not even the best), we have no special quality about us that could lead us to believe that we were specially created by or connected to a Creator God.[18] By taking Earth out of central (albeit very humble) position and casting it into the heavens as one among other planets, Copernicanism implied a connection to Epicurus's cosmology even if Copernicus himself didn't intend it.

If that were not all, we have the difficulty with atomism so forcefully argued by Pietro Redondi in his *Galileo Heretic*: that the real cause of the Church's animus was not Galileo's Copernicanism, but his atomism, because atomism was irreconcilable with the Eucharistic doctrine of transubstantiation.[19] I have resisted bringing up Redondi's well-known but controversial thesis until now to make the point—loud, long, and clear—that there were important, long-standing philosophical and moral objections to atomism independent of any clash with Eucharistic doctrine. I would argue that Redondi goes too far in asserting that *the* cause of Galileo's fateful clash with the Church was that the atomism of *The Assayer* was impossible to reconcile with the Aristotelian-Thomist language of transubstantiation used to sort out what was happening to the bread and wine upon consecration. As Redondi's close argumentation and ample documentation makes clear, however, it was certainly one of the causes.

Redondi's argument is therefore well worth reviewing. That atomism clashes with common sense we have already seen. But think of the difficulty it poses for the orthodox understanding of the change that occurs upon consecration. If all sensible things are mere names—the effect that the substance (literally, the shape) of atoms has on our eyes, tongue, nose, and fingers—then obviously to say with the Church that the bread and wine are changed into Christ but the accidents of the bread and wine (the color, taste, touch, smell) really remain makes no sense at all, since such sensible qualities have no reality but are mere names. Moreover, since atoms are the real substance, the only substance, then how can Jesus Christ really be present in the Host? Does the substance of the bread (atoms) remain alongside the substance of Christ?

Throwing into question the Church's doctrine of the Eucharist was a dangerous thing to do at this time, even if Galileo did it quite accidentally. The Council of Trent had, in the mid-16th century, carefully defined the Holy Eucharist because the new antisacramentalism of most of the Protestant denominations had called it into question. In pushing a view of nature—materialist atomism—that undermined Trent's definition of transubstantiation and, moreover, that could not offer any coherent alternative way in which Christ could be truly present in the Holy Eucharist, Galileo was inadvertently helping those who were already bent on the Church's destruction.

Redondi's argument—based in great part on the discovery of a document that made a formal call for an investigation of Galileo based on the effect of his atomism on the Church's understanding of the Eucharist[20]—is that by giving him a relative slap on the wrist by charging him with promoting Copernicanism after he had promised not to, Pope Urban VIII shielded his friend Galileo from the more devastating charge of heresy against Eucharistic doctrine, for which the punishment would have been quite severe.[21] Whether or not Redondi is right about the intricate workings behind the scenes of the Galileo affair, he is certainly right in emphasizing so strongly and thoroughly the Church's long-standing antagonism to Democritan-Epicurean atomism and the struggles of the Church at the time in dealing with Protestantism as the important larger context of our judgment about it.

Where Does the Church Stand Today?

Obviously, the Church does not stand by its original condemnation of the Copernican theory (although, of course, we have moved far beyond Copernicanism in science). In July 1981, Pope John Paul II set up a commission to study the Galileo affair, on which historians, scientists, and theologians worked for over a decade. In 1992, using the findings of the commission, Pope John Paul II declared that the Church should not have condemned Copernicanism and that the Church had mishandled the Galileo affair. Of course, he was not thereby affirming that the materialism of Galileo's *Assayer* was thereby true or that the dangers of materialism have somehow passed. Nor was the Church now affirming Copernicanism—we know that neither the Earth nor our sun is the center of the universe, and the orbits of planets are not perfectly circular.[22]

But the lessons of the controversy should remain, especially since the Galileo affair is iconic for those pushing the warfare myth. One of the chief lessons is this: the Copernican and Galilean affairs were far more complex than we've been led to believe. The conflicts were not caused by the Church's animosity to science but by the feared implications of the new materialism and of new cosmological possibilities that would take much more time to sort out and digest. The Church was actually siding with the best proponents of science at the time, not attacking reason on behalf of obscurantist faith. Moreover, the sheer absurdity of the claim that what happened to Galileo is somehow iconic of the way that the Church relates to science should now be obvious, given what we covered in the previous chapter. The Church was the great promoter of science in its university curriculum in the centuries before Galileo, at the time of Galileo, and has remained so right down to the present. A single conflict with Galileo does not weigh against all this counterevidence. That the Galileo affair continues to be singled out makes us rightly suspicious that the strong undercurrent of anti-Catholic bias determining the warfare thesis of Draper and White still flows through our culture.

The Fourth Confusion

"The Church Accepts Darwinism" or "The Church Rejects Evolution"

As you might guess from the title, here we have seemingly opposite confusions to deal with: first, that the Church uncritically accepts Darwinism, and second, at the other end of the spectrum, that the Church rejects evolution. If Darwinism and evolution were the same thing, then obviously our chapter title would make no sense at all. How could the Church's position be, at one and the same time, that it rejects Darwinism and accepts evolution if Darwinism and evolution are merely synonymous? But if those two words express a real and important distinction, then it might make sense after all. And in fact, I shall argue that the distinction is not only real but also the key to understanding the Church's approach to evolution. For it is the distinction between a particular view of evolution and evolution itself, between a particular theory and the facts.

To come to the nub of it, the Catholic Church does indeed reject Darwinism and accept evolution, and until we very clearly *see* the difference between the two, we shall have no grasp of the seemingly contradictory way that the Church treats the issue.

But First, a Little Confusion . . .

We might clear things up by first muddying them a bit, putting side by side some statements made by the Church that seem to be contradictory. We return to a very important section of the *Catechism* that we've viewed once before.

> Though faith is above reason, there can never be any real discrepancy between faith and reason. Since the same God who reveals mysteries and infuses faith has bestowed the light of reason on the human mind, God cannot deny himself, nor can truth ever contradict truth. Consequently, methodical research in all branches of knowledge, provided it is carried out in a truly scientific manner and does not override moral laws, can never conflict with the faith, because the things of the world and the things of faith derive from the same God. The humble and persevering investigator of the secrets of nature is being led, as it were, by the hand of God in spite of himself, for it is God, the conserver of all things, who made them what they are. (para. 159)

Now, to bring things to bear on evolution, this should mean that true evolutionary science not only does not but cannot contradict the Faith, that the truths revealed in the Bible and in Church doctrine cannot contradict the facts of evolution, and the facts of evolution cannot contradict revelation. Of course, if such were the case, then one should never find the Church speaking otherwise.

But then I turn, in my *Catechism*, to another interesting passage, where the Church emphatically teaches, "We believe that God created the world according to his wisdom. It is not the product of any necessity whatever, nor of blind fate or chance" (para. 295).

This is not a mere matter of philosophy, but of revealed truth as a previous section makes clear.

> "In the beginning was the Word . . . and the Word was God . . . all things were made through him, and without him was not anything made." The New Testament reveals that God created everything by the eternal Word, his beloved Son. In him "all things were created, in heaven and on Earth . . . all things were created through him and for him. He is before all things, and in him all things hold together." (para. 291)
>
> Scripture and Tradition never cease to teach and celebrate this fundamental truth: "The world was made for the glory of God." (para. 293)

How can this be? If evolution is a science and if its fundamental assumption is that creatures are created by a combination of blind fate or chance, that is, the blind laws of nature or the random jostling of matter and energy, then quite obviously things are *not* created according to God's wisdom, least of all by the eternal Word, God's beloved Son.

A century and a half ago, Charles Darwin himself would seem to have made quite clear that the production of creatures was not a divine act. In his *Origin of Species* we have a most succinct assertion of the way that new species arise from natural selection: "As many more individuals of each species are born than can possibly survive; and as, consequently, there is a frequently recurring struggle for existence, it follows that any being, if it vary however slightly in any manner profitable to itself, under the complex and sometimes varying conditions of life, will have a better chance of surviving, and thus be *naturally selected*. From the strong principle of inheritance, any selected variety will tend to propagate its new and modified form."[1] Here, there is no need for a creator, and there is no wisdom manifest in what evolution produces. As today's most famous spokesman for evolution, Richard Dawkins, so famously puts it, "Natural selection, the blind, unconscious, automatic process which Darwin discovered, and which we now know is the explanation for the existence and apparently purposeful form of all life, has no purpose in mind. It has no mind and no mind's eye. It does not plan for the future. It has no vision, no foresight, no sight at all. If it can be said to play the role of watchmaker in nature, it is the *blind* watchmaker."[2] No one, in reading this, would be surprised to find that Dawkins is also an atheist, and that in his mind, "Darwin made it possible to be an intellectually fulfilled atheist."[3]

So given what we've set out so far, the Church would have to reject evolution. But then it would have to renege on its heady notion that "there can never be any real discrepancy between faith and reason," and hence between faith and science, for the science of evolution, taken as Darwin or Dawkins define it, certainly appears to directly contradict the Church's understanding of purposeful creation.

Dawkins, today's leading Darwinist, certainly thinks so. He defines not just evolution but the science of biology itself as "the study of complicated things that give the *appearance* of having been designed for a purpose."[4]

If Dawkins is right, then at least we know where the Church sits on the issue! It must reject evolution. But does it? Because now I turn a bit further on in my *Catechism* and discover that the Church asserts that "Creation has its own goodness and proper perfection, but it did not spring forth complete from the hands of the Creator. The universe was created 'in a state of journeying' (*in statu viae*) toward an ultimate perfection yet to be attained, to which God has destined it" (para 302). And down a little bit more I find that "with infinite wisdom and goodness God freely willed to create a world 'in a state of journeying' toward its ultimate perfection. In God's plan this process of becoming involves the appearance of certain beings and the disappearance of others, the existence of the more perfect alongside the less perfect, both constructive and destructive forces of nature" (para 310). If that isn't evolution, what is? And if that didn't make things confusing enough, I flip back to a section in the *Catechism* that seems to offer cheerful admiration of the science that Dawkins assumes makes the Creator, at best, an irritating and irrelevant redundancy: "The question about the origins of the world and of man has been the object of many scientific studies which have splendidly enriched our knowledge of the age and dimensions of the cosmos, the development of life-forms and the appearance of man. These discoveries invite us to even greater admiration for the greatness of the Creator, prompting us to give him thanks for all his works and for the understanding of his wisdom he gives to scholars and researchers" (para. 283). Then we drop down a paragraph and find that these sciences (especially the science of biological evolution we presume) lead us to a more fundamental question: "Is the universe governed by chance, blind fate, anonymous necessity, or by a transcendent, intelligent and good Being called 'God?'" (284).

Well, if *that* is the question we must ultimately answer, then we're really in a fix because the very science that leads us to ask it already seems to tell us the answer, and not the one we want to hear: the universe is governed by chance, blind fate, anonymous necessity.

Is there a way out of this seemingly hopeless muddle? Yes, there is. The way begins by first grasping that Darwinism is *a* theory of evolution, a *philosophy* of evolution, a *particular approach* to evolution that assumes that evolution is the result of chance, blind fate, and brute necessity, and explains the evidence for evolution accordingly. So it is quite possible to have a non-Darwinian account of the evidence for evolution; such an account is the only evolutionary theory the Church could accept.

The Theory of Evolution Didn't Begin with Darwin

We can begin to sort things out by turning to history. As I mentioned in the last chapter, the notion of evolution is far older, about two millennia older, than Darwin. It arose first as a particular kind of materialist philosophy. Its first advocates were Epicurus and Lucretius, and their particular doctrine of evolution was that blind chance and material necessity are fully sufficient to explain how it is that all the splendiferous variety of living creatures came about—no Creator need have existed, or be imagined, for the job. As Lucretius put it, in his poetic drama of blind creation, the eternal jostling of atoms can do it all: "Multitudinous atoms, swept along in multitudinous courses through infinite time by mutual clashes and their own weight, have come together in every possible way and tested everything that could be formed by their combinations. So it comes about that a voyage of immense duration, in which they have experienced every variety of movement and conjunction, has at length brought together those whose sudden encounter often forms the starting-point of substantial fabrics—Earth and sea and sky and the races of living creatures."[5] The chance combination of atoms explains everything: how the endless numbers of worlds arose and how on our world, "Even now multitudes of animals are formed out of the Earth with the aid of showers and the sun's genial warmth." Of course, since the process was blind, in the early days of our world,

> the Earth attempted also to produce a host of monsters, grotesque in build and aspect—hermaphrodites, halfway between the sexes yet cut off from either, creatures bereft of feet or dispossessed of hands, dumb, mouthless brutes, or eyeless and blind, or disabled by the adhesion of limbs to the body, so that they could neither

do anything nor go anywhere nor keep out of harm's way nor take what they needed. These and other such monstrous and misshapen births were created. But all in vain. Nature debarred them from increase. They could not gain the coveted flower of maturity nor procure food nor be coupled by the arts of Venus. For it is evident that many contributory factors are essential to be able to forge the chain of a species in procreation.

In those days, again, many species must have died out altogether and failed to forge the chain of offspring. Every species that you now see drawing the breath of life has been protected and preserved from the beginning of the world either by cunning or by courage or by speed. . . . But those gifted with none of these natural assets . . . all these, trapped in the toils of their own destiny, were fair game and an easy prey for others, till nature brought their race to extinction.[6]

Sounds more than a bit like Darwinism, doesn't it? I quote Lucretius at such great length to draw together several important points:

1. Darwin couldn't have "discovered" evolution because the main essentials of his theory are all right here in this first-century-BC Roman Epicurean.
2. This account of evolution was, again, put forward explicitly by Lucretius to convince readers that the heavens and Earth, and all living creatures on the Earth, including human beings, could be entirely explained by the chance association of material atoms over infinite time and space.
3. This account of purely materialist evolution was known to the early Christians, and it was one of the reasons that they so vehemently rejected Epicurean atomism.
4. It was largely through the rediscovery and dissemination throughout Europe of Lucretius's poem in the 15th

through the 18th centuries that the doctrine of evolution became known to Europeans—long before Charles Darwin was born.

All of this makes us aware of a vastly important historical truth: the Church encountered a particular philosophy of evolution long before it encountered any scientific facts that might support evolution, and the particular philosophy was constructed by Epicurus and Lucretius so that (if we might borrow from Richard Dawkins) they and their followers might all be intellectually fulfilled atheists. [7]

The Church in the Time of Darwin

What, then, was the Church's reaction to the appearance of Darwin's famous *Origin of Species* (1859) and his even more provocative *Descent of Man* (1871)? Although the Church judiciously held off saying anything directly and officially about evolution in the 19th century, in the First Vatican Council (1869–70) it made firm its opposition to materialism and to any Epicurean notion that the creation of living things could be understood as an endless set of accidents.

In the Dogmatic Constitution of the Catholic Faith (Session Three) it declared, "There is one true and living God, creator and lord of heaven and Earth" (Ch. 1.1),[8] and that "this one true God, by his goodness and almighty power . . . brought into being from nothing the twofold created order, that is the spiritual and the bodily, the angelic and the earthly, and thereafter the human which is, in a way, common to both since it is composed of spirit and body" (Ch. 1.3). God as creator was affirmed and materialism was rejected. Moreover, this God could "be known with certainty from the consideration of created things, by the natural power of human reason," including, of course, biological things (Ch. 2.1).

The truths we find in nature through science cannot contradict the truths we receive by faith, for "God cannot deny himself, nor can truth ever be in opposition to truth." (Ch. 4.6). But that means "every assertion contrary to the truth of enlightened faith is totally false" (Ch. 4.7), and therefore the Church, as protector of the Faith, has "the right and duty of condemning what wrongly passes for knowledge, lest anyone be led astray by philosophy and empty deceit" (Ch. 4.8). This has direct import for science and scientists, for it means by implication that "all faithful Christians are forbidden to defend as the legitimate conclusions of science those opinions which are known to be contrary to the doctrine of faith, particularly if they have been condemned by the Church; and furthermore they are absolutely bound to hold them to be errors which wear the deceptive appearance of truth" (Ch. 4.9). The Council made clear that the Church does not reject science, but actively promotes it (Ch. 4.11). Scientists are free to use their own proper principles and methods, but the Church "takes particular care that they do not become infected with errors by conflicting with divine teaching, or, by going beyond their proper limits, intrude upon what belongs to faith and engender confusion" (4.12). All to the contrary was declared anathema.[9]

So although the Church said nothing directly about evolution during the initial blooming of Darwinism, nonetheless it

- repeated the understanding that truth cannot contradict truth and so revelation cannot contradict the truths of nature discovered by science;
- set itself directly against materialism and against any view of science that allegedly contradicted its doctrine of creation; it confirmed that it fully supports science but must retain its critical stance toward any philosophy of nature that guides a particular science toward illicit conclusions;
- forbade the faithful from defending as "legitimate

conclusions of science those opinions which are known to be contrary to the doctrine of faith, particularly if they have been condemned by the Church";

• asserted that the faithful—*including scientists*—are bound to hold that conclusions of science contrary to faith are "errors which wear the deceptive appearance of truth."

I refer to the conclusions of this council in such detail because it was the very same one that officially declared that the pope and the council under his guidance could not err; hence, those declarations are infallible. The declaration of their infallibility, we might say, *demands* that Catholics must make a distinction between Darwinism and evolution. So we must get an even better handle on that distinction, and that means we need to look more closely at Darwin himself.

But Was Charles Darwin a Darwinist?

Perhaps we are putting the whole thing wrongly. It may be true that the Church can and must reject a particular ancient form of evolutionary theory, the one originally begotten by Epicurus and Lucretius, the one that influenced many other European thinkers throughout the 15th through the 18th centuries, but that would only mean that the Church must infallibly denounce Epicureans, not Darwinians. If we simply equate Darwinism with the Epicurean version of evolution, then maybe Darwin himself wasn't a Darwinist. Perhaps he was simply a scientist, discovering the hard facts of evolution, entirely unconnected with any philosophical fantasies hatched by Epicurus or Lucretius, and the whole notion of distinguishing between Darwinism and evolution is misconceived.

I have argued long and hard elsewhere that Darwinism is indeed a species of Epicureanism,[10] so here I will only offer a condensed version. One of the most interesting facts to begin with is that

Charles Darwin was not even the first evolutionist in his family. That honor goes to his grandfather Erasmus Darwin, who wrote three works on "transmutationism" (as evolution was first called): the poems in his *Botanic Garden* (1791), the two-volume treatise *Zoönomia* (1794–96), and the poem *The Temple of Nature* (1803)— all of which were penned before Charles was born. Darwin's father, Robert, was also an evolutionist. And whereas Erasmus may have been some kind of a very thin Deist, Robert was an atheist. Erasmus was a leading member of the European radical Enlightenment, known all over Europe and even in America (being an especial friend of Benjamin Franklin). Thus Charles Darwin was born into, and grew up within, a very secularized family: a third-generation evolutionist who imbibed the Lucretian transmutationism of his famous grandfather *long before he ever set foot on the HMS Beagle.*

Why is that last point so important? The common historical "notion" of Darwin's life—what I call the Darwin Myth[11]—is that Charles Darwin was always very religious, and in fact, a kind of biblical literalist, until he sailed around the world on his famous journey on the *Beagle* (1831–36) where he discovered the ancient fossils of dinosaurs and all the geological evidence of an ancient Earth. This, so goes the myth, produced in him a religious crisis. But he just couldn't deny the obvious facts of evolution, and so, after much wrestling and inner turmoil, he finally published his *Origin of Species* in 1859, having become a wise and sober agnostic forced to accept the truth by science itself.

This picture is manifestly false. Not only had Charles read his grandfather's *Zoönomia* before sailing off on the *Beagle* but he had also read the work of the famous French evolutionist, Jean Baptiste Lamarck (who was indebted intellectually to Erasmus Darwin), and worked as an assistant to the radical evolutionist Robert Grant. In fact, he was eagerly reading a book discussing evolution while on board the *Beagle*, less than a year after it set sail. Even more interesting, we know from his secret notebooks, begun almost immediately after disembarking from the *Beagle* in 1836, that Charles Darwin was trying to work out an entirely materialistic account of evolution, one that needed no creator, one that reduced human beings to materialistically determined animals. Obviously he'd been thinking about evolution for a long time before he set sail.

Where did we get the false picture of Darwin? Largely, from Darwin himself, especially from his *Autobiography* where he presents the notion that, again, he was an entirely religious man until the facts of evolution caused him—after much distress—to face the truth. By now, I hope, we can see why Darwin might misrepresent himself: he too shared in the "warfare myth," the idea that history is to be understood as a great conflict in which the hard facts of science force mankind out of its religious infancy and toward its utopian secular, scientific future. As I make clear in *The Darwin Myth*, and as we saw in chapter 1, the warfare thesis had already captivated the leading intellectuals of the 18th-century Enlightenment (Erasmus Darwin being one of them), and set the intellectual stage for the 19th century, Darwin's century. Darwin's theory was part of this larger secular intellectual revolution, of which Charles Darwin's own family had been a part for two generations.

Note the importance of what I am saying: *the particular philosophy came first*. Darwin's approach to evolution was guided by the larger secular Enlightenment in which the Epicurean presentation of evolution had already been firmly embedded by the time he arrived on the scene. Darwin's *theory* of evolution sounds so much like Lucretius's theory of evolution, not because Lucretius was centuries ahead of his time, but because Darwin was deeply imbued with the Epicurean presentation of evolution before he ever gathered a single fact to support it. That is why he came up with a particular view of evolution that excluded God, replacing him by a combination of chance and necessity. The facts didn't drive him to it: that is where he drove the facts.

Evolutionists against Darwinism

If what I'm saying were true, during Darwin's time there would have been *other* attempts to understand the same evolutionary evidence but, in direct contrast to Darwin, attempts that did so in God-friendly ways. It just so happens that there were such attempts, and in fact, they came from Darwin's own friends and supporters.

Why don't we hear about this in our history books and see it on the endless science documentaries on PBS? The answer is quite simple. We are still largely defined, at least the powerful and influential elements of our intellectual culture are largely defined, by the warfare myth, and so such books and documentaries insist on presenting Darwin as *the* only evolutionist, the discoverer of evolution, the man who illustrates the "truth" that science must replace the superstitions of religion.

Who were these God-friendly evolutionists then? Let's begin with Alfred Russel Wallace. As you may know, before Darwin was ready to publish his theory of evolution, he received in the mail a fateful essay by one Alfred Russel Wallace that so clearly and succinctly stated all the basics of Darwin's account of evolution by natural selection that Darwin was both shocked and crestfallen that he'd been scooped. As he was a man of honor, he had to give credit to Wallace, and so, before the *Origin of Species* was published, Wallace became known as the codiscoverer of the theory of evolution by random variation and natural selection. But Wallace, who was every bit the scientist that Darwin was and had done far more exotic and extensive field work, began to have doubts as the 1860s wore on, and in 1869 he published them (much to Darwin's chagrin). In short, Wallace remained an evolutionist even while he took direct issue with Darwin's account of evolution, especially his account of human evolution. His words are well worth quoting.

> Neither natural selection nor the more general theory of evolution can give any account whatever of the origin of

sensational or conscious life. They may teach us how, by chemical, electrical, or higher natural laws, the organized body can be built up, can grow, can reproduce its like; but those laws and that growth cannot even be conceived as endowing the newly-arranged atoms with consciousness. But the moral and higher intellectual nature of man is as unique a phenomenon as was conscious life on its first appearance in the world, and the one is almost as difficult to conceive as originating by any law of evolution as the other. We may even go further, and maintain that there are certain purely physical characteristics of the human race which are not explicable on the theory of variation and survival of the fittest.[12]

In short, the pure materialism of Darwin's God-free theory couldn't explain how life arose and especially was inadequate to explain how the moral and intellectual nature of human beings came about.

Darwin was horrified that Wallace, the codiscoverer of his theory, was now finding it inadequate, and he turned for comfort to his friend, the geologist Charles Lyell, who had done so much to push Darwin's account. But alas, Lyell agreed with Wallace. Furious and frustrated, Darwin set out to show that an entirely Godless account of evolution could indeed explain how human beings got their moral and intellectual nature, and the result was his *Descent of Man* (1871). We'll get to that in a moment.

But first, we should add that the greatest, most formidable opponent to Darwinism—the man whom Darwin himself expended more effort in trying to refute in later editions of the *Origin of Species* than any other critic—was himself an evolutionist (and a convert to Catholicism), St. George Jackson Mivart (the "St." being part of his name, not something added later by the Church!). Mivart had been a pupil of Darwin's secular bulldog and bully pulpit advocate, Thomas Huxley. But like Wallace, he'd come to see the *scientific* problems with a purely materialist account of evolution that tried to explain everything in biological evolution by random variation and natural selection alone. In the same year that Darwin published *Descent of Man*, Mivart published his *On the Genesis of Species*, a theistic account of evolution that subjects Darwin's antitheistic account to the most thorough dissection done in Darwin's lifetime. Wallace then offered his own God-friendly account in 1910: *The World of Life*.[13]

So if history were to be understood properly, without the blinders of the warfare thesis, our understanding of the 19th century, Darwin's century, would be much different. Instead of seeing Darwin as the discoverer of evolution and Darwinism as the only theory of evolution, we would see Darwinism as one species of evolutionary theory that arose to explain the increasing evidence of an ancient Earth and the discovery of a string of exotic fossils of extinct but related living forms. There were other accounts offered—right away—that accepted the evidence of evolution but criticized Darwin's particular account on scientific grounds and offered theistic alternatives.[14] This new and more accurate history would fit with the 19th-century Church's silence about evolution even as it condemned the atheism and materialism that underlay Darwin's account. It would also fit well with the Church's current position of condemning a Darwinian-type account of evolution but in a very general and cautious way, affirming the evidence of evolution. Evolutionary theory didn't have to follow Darwin into the 20th century; it could have followed Wallace, Mivart, and other evolutionists like them. If it had, we would have had a robust theory of theistic evolution and would have avoided a whole host of moral horrors that came packaged with Darwinism. To those we now turn.

The Moral Cost of Darwinism

Another problem with Darwinism, apart from its scientific and philosophical errors, is that it is not just a scientific theory but a moral one. We recall the words of the *Catechism* quoted earlier that "methodical research in all branches of knowledge, provided it is carried out in a truly scientific manner and does not override moral laws, can never conflict with the faith, because the things of the world and the things of faith derive from the same God." Since our moral nature is defined by God, we should never have a conflict between our moral nature and the legitimate findings of science. What if the scientific manner of proceeding wasn't the only problem; what if the science itself, as applied to man, ran roughshod over moral laws? So it did with Darwin.

In *Origin of Species*, Darwin had carefully avoided the topic of human evolution, rightly believing that if he published the purely materialistic account of human origins and human nature, his whole theory would be immediately rejected. What pushed him into showing his entire hand was, again, that his own friends had denied that natural selection alone could explain the moral and intellectual abilities found in human beings. And so, in his *Descent of Man* Darwin set out to apply his theory directly to man, with no quarter given to any hint of theism. The result was shocking—or at least, it should be.

With *Descent*, Darwin earned the title Father of the Modern Eugenic Movement by applying natural selection directly to human beings as the sole source of their abilities. The implication, drawn boldly by Darwin himself, was that in order for mankind to advance intellectually and morally, the less fit had to be eliminated. Two rather unpleasant results followed from this.

First, it implied the eugenic conclusion that preserving the lives of the "less fit" actually worked against the evolutionary progress of humanity. According to Darwin, savages who "obeyed" the

dictates of natural selection were to be admired. For as a consequence, "the weak in body or mind are soon eliminated; and
those that survive commonly exhibit a vigorous state of health."
But civilization brings with it a kind of perverse charity that
undermines the beneficent laws of natural selection by trying to
save the weak. In Darwin's own chilling words,

> We civilised men, on the other hand, do our utmost to
> check the process of elimination; we build asylums for
> the imbecile, the maimed, and the sick; we institute poor-
> laws; and our medical men exert their utmost skill to save
> the life of every one to the last moment. There is rea-
> son to believe that vaccination has preserved thousands,
> who from a weak constitution would formerly have
> succumbed to small-pox. Thus the weak members of
> civilised societies propagate their kind. No one who has
> attended to the breeding of domestic animals will doubt
> that this must be highly injurious to the race of man. It
> is surprising how soon a want of care, or care wrongly
> directed, leads to the degeneration of a domestic race;
> but excepting in the case of man himself, hardly any one
> is so ignorant as to allow his worst animals to breed.[15]

The obvious eugenic implication was that we *should not* allow
the human race to degenerate by interfering with the natural
elimination of the weak, and of course, on the other end, that the
best should breed the most. Darwin shied away from suggesting
the direct elimination of the weak, saying with a sigh that "we
must bear without complaining the undoubtedly bad effects of
the weak surviving and propagating their kind." But at least the
less "fit" could help out by "refraining from marriage."[16] Later
Darwinists would not be so kind.

But there is another important implication of asserting that
morality is the result of natural selection (and not from our being

made in the image of God): it means that morality is reducible to whatever contributes to a particular individual's or society's survival. Or to put it the other way around, if a society survived, it must by definition be more fit. Therefore, the particular laws, customs, or beliefs that contributed to its survival, no matter how barbarous or brutal, must be considered "moral"—an interesting twist on Epicurus, with Darwin substituting the identity of goodness with brutality for the hedonist identity of goodness with physical pleasure. In fact, the actual source of morality for Darwin, the actual reason for its rise and development, is the brutal struggle to survive where the less morally fit individuals and races are extinguished by the more morally fit individuals and races. Here's how it works, according to Darwin:

> When two tribes of primeval man, living in the same country, came into competition, if the one tribe included . . . a greater number of courageous, sympathetic, and faithful members, who were always ready to warn each other of danger, to aid and defend each other, this tribe would without doubt succeed best and conquer the other . . . A tribe possessing the above qualities in a high degree would spread and be victorious over other tribes; but in the course of time it would, judging from all past history, be in its turn overcome by some other and still more highly endowed tribe. Thus the social and moral qualities would tend slowly to advance and be diffused throughout the world.[17]

Moral advance comes about through the destruction and hence extinction of the less moral. The same is true, Darwin argues, for intellectual advance.

And this advance through extinction of the "less favored races" is not something that we leave behind in our dark past, even though we have it to thank for our moral, social, cultural, and intellectual progress so far, but something that is now occurring and will continue indefinitely into the future. That is why Darwin could blithely describe the following in the voice of utmost scientific detachment and candor: "At some future period, not very distant as measured by centuries, the civilised races of man will almost certainly exterminate and replace throughout the world the savage races. At the same time the anthropomorphous apes [like the gorilla, orangutan, or chimpanzee] . . . will no doubt be exterminated. The break will then be rendered wider, for it will intervene between man in a more civilised state, as we may hope, than the Caucasian, and some ape as low as a baboon, instead of as at present between the negro or Australian and the gorilla."[18] Civilization progresses by the purposeful extinction of the less-fit races. That is how human evolution worked in the past. The extinction of closely allied species is how the significant gap between existing apes and existing human beings became so large—the "intermediate species" were eliminated. And that is how evolution shall continue to "progress."

Now we must point out here, since this is so monstrous, that Charles Darwin himself was no monster. In fact, he was a most amiable, humble, and personally moral man, a very good husband and father, and a very kind gentleman to the less privileged. He was also an abolitionist who hated slavery with a passion.[19] But all these wonderful things about Charles Darwin the person are in direct and real conflict with the implications of his theory, implications that even he drew out, implications *that followed directly from his insistence that human evolution must be entirely explained as the result of random variation and natural selection*—that is, *without God*.[20]

Quite obviously, the Church cannot endorse this particular view of evolution, and we needn't belabor the point by citing text after text in the *Catechism* to prove it. Our larger point is that this particular view of evolution is rightly called Darwinism (as we have just seen) and it is rightly rejected, but it is not the only view possible, as we have seen even in Darwin's own time with Mivart and Wallace. Along with Mivart and Wallace, who both rejected Darwin's account in part because it couldn't explain the moral and intellectual capacities of human beings, we too can make the fundamental distinction between Darwinism and evolution.

What Does That Mean for the Church Today?

Given this important distinction between Darwinism and evolution, it should not surprise us that Pope Pius XII, in his 1950 encyclical *Humani Generis*, could warn against the dangers of a materialist view of evolution,[21] but then go on to say

the Teaching Authority of the Church does not forbid that, in conformity with the present state of human sciences and sacred theology, research and discussions, on the part of men experienced in both fields, take place with regard to the doctrine of evolution, in as far as it inquires into the origin of the human body as coming from preexistent and living matter—for the Catholic faith obliges us to hold that souls are immediately created by God. However this must be done in such a way that the reasons for both opinions, that is, those favorable and those unfavorable to evolution, be weighed and judged with the necessary seriousness, moderation and measure, and provided that all are prepared to submit to the judgment of the Church, to whom Christ has given the mission of interpreting authentically the Sacred Scriptures and of defending the dogmas of faithful. Some however, rashly transgress this liberty of discussion, when they act as if the origin of the human body from preexisting and living matter were already completely certain and proved by the facts which have been discovered up to now and by reasoning on those facts, and as if there were nothing in the

sources of divine revelation which demands the greatest
moderation and caution in this question. (Section 36)

In other words, the Church did not forbid discussion of evolution but asked that every side of the question, including those
legitimately critical, would be brought to bear. The pope only
forbade materialism's denial of the soul, and in the consequent
paragraph (37), any notion that human ancestry could be derived
from multiple lines (polygenism).

Obviously much evidence for evolution was gathered in the
time between Darwin and Pope Pius XII, and much more has
been gathered down to the present day. We know that the Earth is
about four-and-a-half billion years old; we know that the first living cells (single-celled microbes, lacking internal structures such
as the nucleus, called (prokaryotes, single-celled microbes that
lack internal structures such as the nucleus) appeared on Earth
almost four billion years ago including the nucleus (called eukaryotes), appeared later, perhaps even as late as two billion years
ago. We know that life remained on a relatively simple level until
about 550 million years ago, from which time forward the fossil
record reveals a developing diversification of creatures: from the
first shelled organisms to vertebrates to plants to insects to dinosaurs to reptiles to mammals. Finally, we find stone figures made
by human hands some 40,000 years ago and painting on caves
about 32,000 years ago. The appearance of such a range and
diversity of extinct creatures provides ample evidence that the
development of life has been a very long and very rich process,
one that involved countless extinctions of species that, prior to
the 19th century, no human knew existed—and that seems to
include races of human or humanlike creatures that no longer
exist, such as the Neanderthals. But again, this gradual unfolding
of life needn't be explained on Darwinian terms.

Moreover, there are aspects of the effects of evolutionary
change (whatever their causes) that are firmly established, such

as the appearance of new, closely related species over time in particular geographical areas, for example, the multiple species of the honeycreepers of Hawaii all developing from a finch-like ancestor, or the 500 species of fruit flies that have developed over a period of about eight million years from a common ancestor on Hawaii; the common correspondence in the succession of extinct and living forms in particular geographical areas, such as the pygmy armadillo and the extinct glyptodont in Argentina, or the extinct Australian mammal *Diprotodon* and the wombat; the existence of distinct species in the same area or contiguous areas that differ only slightly, such as the multiple kinds of sparrows; the evidence for the slow change of definite traits in one species over millions of years found in successive geological layers, such as the number of chambers in the marine foraminiferan *Globorotalia conidea* or the number of ribs in trilobites; or the existence of so-called pseudogenes in the genetic code that no longer function but are traceable to functional genes in other species, such as the pseudogene GLO used in making vitamin C from glucose, which most mammals have in functional form but other mammals (primates, fruit bats, and guinea pigs) that get vitamin C from their diets don't.

It is not surprising, therefore, that popes after Pius XII have affirmed evolution even while rejecting Darwinian-type theories. When Pope John Paul II famously stated, in his Message to the Members of the Pontifical Academy of Sciences (October 22, 1996), that "new knowledge has led to the recognition of the theory of evolution as more than a hypothesis" (Section 4), he can only be understood to be following Pope Pius and affirming those aspects of evolutionary biology that were legitimate and non-Darwinian. As he made clear in the same section, there are really "several theories of evolution" in part based on "the various philosophies" underlying them, hence the existence of materialist, reductionist and spiritualist interpretations. He then rejected the materialist and reductionist version—the very version we find in Darwin—and all versions that "consider the mind as emerging from the forces of living matter, or as a mere epiphenomenon of matter," for these are "incompatible with the truth about man" (Section 5). I don't think it's a stretch to suggest that Pope John Paul II would have rejected Darwin's account of "morality."

In Pope Benedict XVI's address at the inauguration of his pontificate in April 2005, he proclaimed, loud and clear, "We are not some casual and meaningless product of evolution."[22] In his 2007 encyclical on the theological virtue of hope, *Spe Salvi*, the pope (in commenting on St. Paul's Letter to the Corinthians), wrote, "It is not the elemental spirits of the universe, the laws of matter, which ultimately govern the world and mankind, but a personal God governs the stars, that is, the universe; it is not the laws of matter and of evolution that have the final say, but reason, will, love—a Person."[23] But Benedict is not rejecting evolution wholesale, as he also has made clear. It is not a matter of either evolution *or* faith, as many would have it in the current debates.

Currently, I see in Germany, but also in the United States, a somewhat fierce debate raging between so-called "creationism" and evolutionism, presented as though they were mutually exclusive alternatives: those who believe in the Creator would not be able to conceive of evolution, and those who instead support evolution would have to exclude God. This antithesis is absurd because, on the one hand, there are so many scientific proofs in favor of evolution which appears to be a reality we can see and which enriches our knowledge of life and being as such. But on the other, the doctrine of evolution does not answer every query, especially the great philosophical question: where does everything come from? And how did everything start which ultimately led to man?[24]

In his book on Genesis, written before becoming pope, Cardinal Ratzinger wrote,

> We cannot say: creation *or* evolution, inasmuch as these two things respond to two different realities. The story of the dust of the Earth and the breath of God [portrayed in Genesis] . . . does not in fact explain how human persons come to be but rather what they are. It explains their inmost origin and casts light on the project that they are. And, vice versa, the theory of evolution seeks to understand and describe biological developments. But in so doing it cannot explain where the "project" of human persons comes from, nor their inner origin, nor their particular nature. To that extent we are faced here with two complementary—rather mutually exclusive—realities.[25]

Pope Benedict affirmed this understanding in the special conference with his former students in 2006 that resulted in the publication of *Creation and Evolution: A Conference with Pope Benedict XVI in Castel Gondolfo.* In it, Pope Benedict confirmed what he had said before, but an often overlooked distinction in his understanding was brought out more clearly by Christoph Cardinal Schönborn, archbishop of Vienna: the distinction between Darwinian evolutionism and evolution, between the ideological, materialistic, reductionist approach to evolution and the facts themselves: "The possibility that the Creator also makes use of the instrument of evolution is admissible for the Catholic faith. The question, though, is whether evolutionism (as an ideological concept) is compatible with a belief in a Creator. The question presupposes, again, that a distinction is made between the scientific theory of evolution and the ideological or philosophical interpretations thereof."[26] This conference was called as the result of the worldwide brouhaha caused by an essay by Cardinal

Schönborn, "Finding Design in Nature," that appeared in the *New York Times* in July 2005.[27] In it, the cardinal stated,

> The Catholic Church, while leaving to science many details about the history of life on Earth, proclaims that by the light of reason the human intellect can readily and clearly discern purpose and design in the natural world, including the world of living things.
>
> Evolution in the sense of common ancestry might be true, but evolution in the neo-Darwinian sense—an unguided, unplanned process of random variation and natural selection—is not. Any system of thought that denies or seeks to explain away the overwhelming evidence for design in biology is ideology, not science.

But, alas, the world could not understand the Cardinal's important distinction between evolutionism (or neo-Darwinism as he calls it here) and the facts of evolution understood without materialist, reductionist blinders. In order to clarify these brief statements, Cardinal Schönborn devoted his monthly catechetical lectures of the academic year 2005–6 to a deep elaboration of the Church's position, published in book form as *Chance or Purpose? Creation, Evolution, and a Rational Faith*.[28] This book remains the most up-to-date reflections about the essential distinction between Darwinism, on the one hand, and the legitimate science of evolution on the other.

So . . . What's a Good Catholic to Believe?

"So," the reader might well ponder, "now what? What *exactly* is a good Catholic supposed to believe about evolution?" This is a question I always get. But the answer is not at all simple.

First of all, a good Catholic must reject Darwinism, and not identify it simply with evolution. Identifying the two leads to two unpleasant and opposite results. First, those who accept evolution believe that they must then either reject God or somehow incongruously weld together a theory of evolution meant to displace the Creator and a Creator with nothing to do. Second, those who rightly reject Darwinism will, quite mistakenly, reject the facts of evolution as part of the poison. The first leads to atheism, the second to irrational fideism. Neither alternative is Catholic.

A good Catholic must be very patient. For a century and a half, evolutionary science has largely, almost exclusively, been advancing its work within the materialistic, reductionist framework of Darwinism. That means that it has attempted to gather all its evidence under the assumption that evolution is an entirely blind process governed by blind laws. Just like a Marxist historian who only gathers evidence that supports his thesis that all human activity, thought, and creation are reducible to the historical modes of production and the class conflict that results therefrom, so also Darwinists have only looked for what they wanted to find—evidence that evolution is an entirely undirected, Godless process. It should not surprise us that evolutionary biology, as it exists now, only offers evidence for Darwinism. In order to reverse this long-standing trend, scientists will have to cast off the blinders of philosophical materialism and allow their reason to look at evidence for evolution in a new, brighter, more expansive light. Until that occurs—and continues for some time, say a half-century—we won't know what exactly to believe about evolution. We need to think in Church years, and hence the need for patience.

A good Catholic can recognize what we've outlined from the very beginning about the place of the Church. The Church has affirmed evolution in a very broad way once the evidence from nature proved overwhelming, and it did so because the evidence of God's creating activity in nature cannot contradict the Faith. Of this we must be confident, or we will become a new kind of Manichean, dividing salvation in the spiritual realm from our understanding of creation. But the Church also takes seriously its task of protecting science from bad philosophy, even while it does not dictate the particulars of any science.

Are there any promising approaches to evolution out there? Yes, I would say that evolutionary paleobiologist Simon Conway Morris is, more or less, on the right track. Morris is a first-class scientist with everyone's respect, and on top of that, a believing Christian (with a deep, incurable love of reading G. K. Chesterton). Moreover, he has no patience with the cant and shoddy reasoning of rabidly antitheistic Darwinists like Richard Dawkins. His *Life's Solution* is a good place to start.[29] Of course, every Catholic should read the aforementioned book by Pope Benedict, *"In the Beginning...": A Catholic Understanding of the Story of Creation and the Fall*, Cardinal Schönborn's *Chance or Purpose? Creation, Evolution, and a Rational Faith*, and the proceedings from the conference on evolution and creation, *Creation and Evolution: A Conference with Pope Benedict XVI in Castel Gondolfo*.

Readers interested in going into more detail about evolution will have to do some exploring in enemy territory, as it were, and that means having to sort out the reasonable claims from ideological Darwinism. So be prepared! First of all, and most obvious, watch out for scientists (such as Richard Dawkins and Jerry Coyne) who seem to continually gravitate toward antireligious statements in the midst of evolutionary arguments. They have a bone to pick with theists that heavily slants how they gather and present evidence. Second, and equally important, keep in mind the distinction between a reductionist Darwinian explanation and a solid and sober description of the facts. A reductionist explanation tries to force evolution to be explained entirely as the result of random variations, natural selection, and a few other factors, and the result is often that near-miracles are continually invoked to explain why there are large gaps in the fossil record, how dauntingly complex organs can evolve, or how certain kinds of evolution occur with uncanny rapidity. If you continually encounter the near-miraculous in an evolutionary account, then it is a sign the author is invoking *chance* as a counterdeity. A theistic explanation, by contrast, has far less trouble because it assumes that the universe is designed for the development of complex life, and so it doesn't need to bend facts to make them fit the Darwinian framework. In the next two chapters, we will examine the evidence that the universe is, indeed, strangely and wonderfully designed for life.

THE FIFTH CONFUSION

"The Big Bang Is a Scientific Alternative to Belief in a Creator God"

Most people for most of human history have believed that the universe had a definite beginning in time—when it was created by God or the gods. So it may seem strange that it came as such a shock, in the first half of the 20th century, for scientists to *discover* that the universe had a beginning.

To make a very long and complicated story too short, the cause of the shock was that scientists had been certain that the universe was in fact eternal. It *had* to be. Why? For two related reasons.

First, we must return to Epicurus and Lucretius, whose influence on the early development of modern science cannot be overestimated. An essential part of their theory was that both the universe and atoms were eternal—that they had *always* existed, and thus did not need a creator. No more bothersome gods! "The totality [of things] has always been just like it is now and always will be," atoms are "unchangeable," and they "move continuously for all time" creating in an infinite, eternal universe, world after world by their random jostlings, couplings, and uncouplings.[1]

Lucretius, too, was zealous to remove the "dead weight of superstition" which he also believed was the cause of all human wickedness and misery. (The ancient roots of the warfare thesis!) So he decided that his "starting point" should be this: "*Nothing is ever created by divine power out of nothing.*" Since there is no divine creator, nature itself must be eternal, because if it weren't eternal, then it would have to have a beginning in time and nature would have had to create atoms out of nothing. But that is impossible, so . . . the universe and atoms are eternal.[2]

Note the circular reasoning: "We don't want a creator god, so the universe and atoms *must be* eternal; if they weren't eternal, they would have had a beginning; but if they had a beginning, they would have to have come from nothing; but nothing cannot be a cause of something; therefore the universe and atoms must be eternal; consequently, there was no creator god." The only reason the universe and its atoms are "proven" to be eternal is that, if they were not, we'd have to invoke a creator—the very conclusion Epicurus and Lucretius wanted to avoid at all costs, even at the cost of logic! This circular Epicurean-Lucretian reasoning fed the fires of secularism in the 19th and early 20th century.

But there is another, closely related reason the universe "became" eternal for modernity—Newton's spectacularly successful theories. Isaac Newton made the basics of Epicurean atomism the foundation of his theory of nature found in his justly famous *Philosophiae Naturalis Principia Mathematica* (*Mathematical Principles of Natural Philosophy*, 1687), but Newton himself was very religious (after his own fashion—he seems to have been a kind of Arian). He wouldn't allow his Epicurean atoms to replace the need for the creator God of Genesis. Thus, in his immensely influential *Opticks* (1704), Newton proposed that "it seems probable to me that God in the Beginning form'd Matter in solid, massy, hard, impenetrable, moveable Particles, of such Sizes and Figures, and with such other Properties, and in such Proportion to Space, as most conduced to the End for which he form'd them; and that these primitive Particles being Solids, are incomparably harder than any porous Bodies compounded of them, even so very hard as never to wear or break into pieces; no ordinary Power being able to divide what God himself made one in the first Creation."[3] Newton's atoms were everlasting, like those of Epicurus, but Newton asserted that they were *created* that way rather than having always existed. Furthermore, against Epicureanism, these particles didn't bang about randomly, but were "variously associated in the first Creation by the Counsel of an intelligent Agent. For it became Him who created them to set them in order. And if He did so, it's unphilosophical to seek for any other Origin of the World, or to pretend that it might arise out of Chaos by the mere Laws of Nature; though being once form'd, it may continue by those Laws for many Ages."[4]

Whatever we make of his account of the creation of atoms, Newton's account of the physics of motion was brilliant, and Newtonianism defined science from its inception at the very end of the 17th century up until the beginning of the 20th. However, with the advent of Darwinism in the 19th century, it became quite "philosophical" to believe that everything could "arise out of Chaos by the mere Laws of Nature" through the random association of atoms. A godless Newtonianism coupled with Darwinism gave scientists license to accept an eternal universe *sans* Creator.

At the dawn of the 20th century, cracks started to appear in Newton's world, and a new science, defined by Einstein's theory of relativity, arose. One of the strange things that his theory entailed—a thing Einstein did not like at all—was that, if it were right, the universe would be expanding, and if it were expanding, then if one ran the tape backward, so to speak, space, time, and matter would all contract on an infinitely dense "singularity." That metaphorical "point" would imply that time, space, and matter, and that laws of nature that govern them, *burst into existence from nothing.* Indeed, it was in 1927 that a Belgian Jesuit priest named Georges Lemaître announced that if Einstein's theory was right, one had to conclude that the universe was expanding, and that it therefore was neither eternal nor infinite but had a definite, calculable beginning.

For Lemaître, unlike Einstein, these implications of the latest science "had strong theological relevance . . . An initial singularity was not something to be avoided, but a positive merit, a token of God's creation of the world."[5] Meanwhile, Edwin Hubble declared in 1929 that distant galaxies did, in fact, seem to be moving away from us and each other at incredible speeds (as evidenced in what is called the red shift, where light waves moving away from us appear red because the waves are "stretched out" to a lower frequency). As the century unfolded, more and more evidence pointed to the conclusion: the universe was not eternal, so it must have had a beginning.

"Big Bang" was not the name originally given to this event. The tag was applied, so the story goes, in 1949 by the astronomer Fred Hoyle, an agnostic. This is quite interesting, because Hoyle was, like Einstein, originally put off by the notion that the universe had a definite beginning, and in fact developed the "steady state" theory in direct opposition to it. Hoyle's theory was an elaborate variation of the Epicurean eternal universe, wherein the universe itself continues to create new matter as it expands. But even Hoyle eventually had to give in. The evidence all pointed to the Big Bang.

Hoyle later discovered something even stranger about this "Bang." If it was actually something like an explosion, it was an extraordinarily well-orchestrated, finely tuned one. In simply following out the evidence, Hoyle realized that in order for carbon atoms to be produced through stellar evolutionary processes, what is called the "nuclear resonance" of carbon would have to be unimaginably exact. Since carbon is the basic biological building block, the startling precision had implications for chemistry and biology as well as physics. Hoyle famously remarked, "A commonsense interpretation of the facts suggests that a super intellect has monkeyed with physics, as well as chemistry and biology, and that there are no blind forces worth speaking about in nature."[6]

If there were only a single instance of such fine-tuning, then we might dismiss it; but since the latter part of the 20th century, scientists have found example after example. The universe isn't eternal, and the Big Bang looks suspiciously like an extremely well-planned Big Bloom. How well planned?

Fine-Tuning and the Big Bloom

As long as scientists could hold to an eternal, infinite universe with eternal atoms moving about randomly in it, the basic Epicurean secularist cosmology could remain intact. You didn't need a creator. You could simply imagine that, with infinite time and space and infinite matter moving about in it, random creation of multiple worlds was not only possible but inevitable. The discovery of the "Big Bang" brought an end to this easy speculation, for by calculating backward, using the speeds at which galaxies were hurtling away from each other, scientists could with fair accuracy determine the beginning of space, matter, and time itself—around 13 billion years ago.

The calculation of a beginning point to the universe introduced another deadly serious difficulty for the secular-minded: it meant that the universe had to develop. Atoms didn't just pop into existence; rather, all the distinct chemical elements from hydrogen, helium, lithium, beryllium, boron, carbon, nitrogen, oxygen, on up had to develop over time, step by step, through a very exact process. And it was in this building up of all the chemical elements necessary for life that scientists kept finding ever more fantastic examples of fine-tuning.

We have already mentioned the extraordinary exactitude of carbon resonance. But we must go back even further in time before chemical elements could even develop. As we now know, atoms are not just Epicurean blobs. Each of the atomic elements has an elaborate subatomic structure, consisting of electrons, protons, and neutrons (and even stranger things beyond and below). Protons, as we learned in high school chemistry, are the positively charged particles in an atom's nucleus. Each successive element, beginning from hydrogen, has one more proton in the nucleus. But as we know from magnets, two positive charges repel. So how do the protons stick together in the nucleus? By what is called the strong nuclear force. If we changed the strength of this nuclear force just the smallest bit, the universe as we know it would not exist. If the force were a wee bit weaker, it couldn't overcome the repulsive positive force of the protons, and atoms larger than hydrogen couldn't form. You'd have a lifeless, largely formless universe full of hydrogen soup.

The same kind of thing happens with the other major forces of nature: the weak force, gravity, and electromagnetism. Each one must be very precisely designated and calibrated to the other forces, or the simplest chemical elements could not be built up. Since the more complex elements are built from the simpler, the chemical complexity necessary for life would never develop if any of the forces were even the slightest bit different. Yet there is no reason they have to have the precise values they do. They could vary along an enormous range.

Other strange "coincidences" exist. The proton has just a little less mass than the neutron (since its quarks are a bit lighter). If it were just a little bit heavier, we wouldn't even have hydrogen because the protons would then be unstable. Although there may have been heavier elements, without hydrogen there wouldn't be any water and hence there wouldn't be any life. Or change the value of v (in particle physics, the "vacuum expectation value of the Higgs field"), and you ruin any prospects for life. Fiddle with Λ (the "Cosmological Constant" represented by the Greek letter *lambda*), one of the constants governing gravity, and either the entire history of the universe would be collapsed into the smallest fraction of time possible or the expansion of the universe would be so fantastically speedy that no stars, galaxies, and planets could form. Somewhat the same thing happens if we'd try to change the spatial curvature of the universe.[7]

The web of interconnected fine-tuning is so stunningly precise that scientists are often at a loss for words to make it understandable to the nonexpert. "The precision," astrophysicist Michael Turner has tried to explain, "is as if one could throw a dart across the entire universe and hit a bull's-eye one millimeter in diameter on the other side."[8] It is beyond the scope of this book to go into the amazing array of scientific discoveries that confirm instance after instance of fine-tuning at the origin and during the development of our universe, but a number of excellent books, written by a range of scientists and laymen, nontheist and theist, have come out over the last quarter century, and they are well worth the read for those interested in the scientific details.[9]

That the unfolding of the universe is marked by extraordinary fine-tuning is now incontestable, and more evidence is being gathered all the time. There is nothing random about super-precise fine-tuning. Such exactitude is the very opposite of the unintelligent meandering of chance. Coupled with the fact that we know the universe had a definite beginning, all things would seem to point to an intelligent creator.

Escaping from God in Other Universes?

But a strange reaction has set in. There has arisen, within the physics community, the notion that both the evidence of fine-tuning and the fact that our universe had a definite beginning can be gotten around by supposing that *this* universe is the one lucky universe among many—the so-called multiverse theory. The notion goes something like this: "Sure, it *appears* that the universe is so finely tuned that it must have a creator, but that's because we *happen* to live in the one universe that turned out well. Most of the other universes, where all the parameters of physical forces and laws in nature varied among an enormous range, ended up as duds. But given the infinite number of universes being born, it's no surprise that at least one of them (ours!) would come up with the lucky calibration of forces and physical laws. Of course, if there are infinite universes, then surely countless others must also have been so fortunate." So we arrive again at something like the Epicurean view of multiple worlds, only this time it is multiple—infinite—universes, many of which teem with life, and we got there through something like Darwinian random variation and survival of the fittest, as applied to universes rather than biological species.

One obvious problem[10] with the multiverse theory, as many have pointed out, is that there is no evidence for the existence of other universes, and in fact, since we can only observe our own universe, *there is no possible way to get any evidence*. For proponents of the multiverse theory, that means, happily, that we also don't have any way to get evidence *against* them (and some even claim that *every possible universe* actually does exist, either successively or all at once in parallel universes). The most we can say is that multiple universes *might* be possible (for example, if the universe expanded very rapidly at the beginning it might be possible that different "bubbles" of expansion branched off, each creating its own expanding universe), but the existence of such universes is neither necessary in order to explain anything about this universe nor susceptible of any proof. Without assuming bad faith unnecessarily, the multiverse theory certainly seems like a theoretical creation made specifically to get around the fact that *this* universe, the only one we can know, did have a definite beginning and its construction is intimately fine-tuned. In other words, multiverse theory gives every appearance of having been contrived by those who, like Epicurus and Lucretius, are desperate to find a way around God.

Fine-Tuning All the Way Down

The fine-tuning that occurred at the origin of the universe should be enough to overturn the notion that the universe was randomly contrived. But as scientists are finding out in ever more detail, there is fine-tuning *all the way down*, that is, from the very beginning all the way to the foundation of conditions for complex biological life on Earth. And the single most important lesson of science learned over the last 25 years is that those conditions are exacting. Life ain't easy.

Biology depends on a rich chemistry. Contrary to what you may have seen or read in science fiction, you can't have creatures made only of hydrogen. The biological complexity of the human being requires at least 27 elements—we're not even counting the "supporting" elements necessary for a viable world in which to live. Our periodic table of elements, with its array of over 100 chemical elements, is the result of many billions of years of stellar evolution, where successive generations of stars slowly "cooked up" the great feast of elements available on our periodic table. Half of the age of the universe—about seven billion years—was necessary for stellar evolution to produce the needed chemical elements for life. The obvious implication being that life was impossible beforehand, so life is not possible any old time in the universe's history.

Granted life can't arise just *any time*—but can't life happen *anywhere* in space? There are billions and billions of galaxies, each with billions and billions of stars or "suns," so it would certainly seem like the universe should be littered with good real estate. But it's not so. Galaxies come in different types, and a large proportion of the galaxies are completely uninhabitable. We live in a spiral galaxy, the Milky Way, rich enough in chemical elements and orderly enough for life to exist, but the same is not true for an older element-poor elliptical galaxy or an irregular galaxy. Even within our own galaxy, most of the stars couldn't host a habitable planet. Things are far too dangerous in the inner parts of the galaxy, where the stars are densely packed and radiation levels are lethal, and on the outer edge of the galaxy there aren't enough chemical elements. There is only a thin zone of habitability, called the Galactic Habitable Zone, that is far enough out from the center but not too far out.[11]

And will just any star do for a sun? As it turns out, no. There are all kinds of stars, and only a small number are legitimate candidates. Most are too old, too young, too small, too large, too element-poor, too element-rich, too close to other stars, in the wrong place in a good galaxy, in a bad galaxy, and so on. Our sun is exceptional, rather than ordinary.

And what about our Earth? The same thing is true—even more so. We have a solar system of eight or nine planets (depending on whether you agree with Pluto's recent downgrading). Contrary to the reveries of science fictionarians, only the Earth is inhabited, and only the Earth is habitable by complex life (very primitive life may have been possible on Mars). There is a whole host of very exacting conditions necessary for complex life: as with a habitable solar system, a habitable planet has to be just the right distance from its sun; there must be an atmosphere and it must be of a certain chemical makeup; the planet cannot be too large or too small; it must have an active volcanically driven plate tectonic system to continually recirculate the elements necessary for life near the surface; it must have a sufficient amount and variety of chemical compounds in its crust; it must have just the right tilt and spin; there must be sufficient water (but not too much); and on and on.[12]

I have mentioned only a mere fraction of the delicate circumstances and necessary conditions for complex life. As with the fine-tuning of the Big Bang, more are being discovered all the time. The more we know about life, the more we realize how difficult and exacting are the conditions that allow it to begin, and even more, sustain it over long enough times to develop. With every new condition discovered, we eliminate more and more times and places in the universe when and where life could exist. Moreover, we realize ever more deeply, through science, how extraordinary Earth is. The just-rightness of the universe and the just-rightness of Earth should begin to make us suspicious—especially because of the way that they fit together. The just-rightness, or fine-tuning, of the universe's initial condition allowed for there even being a universe—no small feat! But that doesn't mean that life will then pop up everywhere. Almost the entire universe is inhospitable to life. Our galaxy, our solar system, and our Earth are the exception, not the rule.

To make things even more astounding, we must remember that necessary conditions are not *sufficient* conditions. Imagine the set of conditions that allow for complex biological life as a kind of pyramid with a broad base moving up to a peak, level by level. Just because you have the right kind of star doesn't mean that you'll automatically have the right kind or right number of planets orbiting it. Just because you have a planet of the right size at the right distance from the right kind of star in the right kind of galaxy, doesn't mean that it will have the right kind of atmosphere. As we move up the pyramid of conditions, each new level necessitates a further fine-tuning of conditions that is not caused by the level below it. And so the farther up the pyramid we go—that is, the closer we come to the complex set of inter-related conditions that we enjoy on Earth—the more difficult it is to achieve the next level. It's hard to get the right kind of sun, but it's harder still to get the right kind of sun and the size planet orbiting it at the right distance with the right kind of orbit; it's hard to get the right size and position of a planet from the right kind of sun, but it's harder still to get all that plus the right kind of atmosphere; it's hard to get an atmosphere with oxygen, but harder still to get it with the right amount of oxygen.

Now, of course, we've only been talking about the conditions necessary for life, not the appearance of life itself—that we'll talk about in the next chapter. But we've said enough here to make some general and very important conclusions about the Big Bang and what the Church might make of it.

What Does the Church Make of It All?

The Catholic Church does not take an official position on the Big Bang, just as it doesn't wed itself to the particulars of any other developing theory. The reasons should be clear: as we noted in the first chapter, the Church is not in the business of working through the details of any particular science. As we have seen, perhaps the most important scientist in the early development of the theory was a Catholic priest, Georges Lemaître. Pope Pius XII thought that—as against the notion of an eternal universe held to so dearly by secular scientists of the time—the Big Bang affirmed the Church's belief that creation had a beginning in time.[13] Obviously, since the Church has no larger philosophical or theological problems with the theory, it has no difficulty accepting a 13-billion-year-old universe and an Earth that's about four and a half billion years old. Nor does it consider the Big Bang to be in conflict with Scripture, since the Catholic Church does not take a strictly literalist approach to interpreting the Bible. And finally, there's just too much scientific evidence of an old Earth and a finite but old universe. Since the Church firmly believes that the God of Scripture and the God of Creation are the same God, then it must accept the scientific evidence as evidence of God *as* Creator. Cardinal Schönborn has given us the most straightforward answer as to where the Church stands.

> Often nowadays in polemics, belief in creation is lumped together with "creationism." Yet believing in God the Creator is not identical with the way that, in some Christian circles, people try to understand the six days of creation

spoken of the first chapter of the Book of Genesis as if this had been literally reported, as six chronological days, and try by all possible arguments, even scientific ones, to prove that the Earth is about six thousand years old.

The Catholic position on "creationism" is clear. Saint Thomas Aquinas says that one should "not try to defend the Christian faith with arguments that make it ridiculous, because they are in obvious contradiction to reason." It is nonsense to maintain that the world is only six thousand years old. An attempt to prove such a notion scientifically means provoking what Saint Thomas calls the *irrisio infidelium*, the mockery of unbelievers. Exposing the faith to mockery with false arguments of this kind is not right; indeed, it is explicitly to be rejected.[14]

Immediately after stating this, Cardinal Schönborn takes up the evidence for the Big Bang, and does so in the exact manner that the Catholic Church approaches all science: respectfully but critically, guarding especially against any attempts to put a materialistic, atheistic spin on the evidence, and placing the whole discussion in the context of the Church's Catechesis on Creation (Sections 282–324 of the *Catechism*).

It is of signal importance that Cardinal Schönborn places particular emphasis on the fine-tuning of the original conditions and first moments of the Big Bang as evidence for the obvious inference that it could not have happened by chance, referring in particular to physicist Walter Thirring's *Cosmic Impressions: Traces of God in the Laws of Nature*.[15] The cardinal goes on to assert, using the authority of the *Catechism*, that evidence for fine-tuning is legitimate rational, scientific evidence pointing to the existence of God through His creation. The section of the *Catechism* he quotes is noteworthy: "Human intelligence is surely already capable of finding a response to the question of origins. The existence of God the Creator can be known with certainty through his works, by the light of human reason, even if this knowledge is often obscured and disfigured by error. That is why faith comes to confirm and enlighten reason in the correct understanding of this truth."[16] In the footnote, Cardinal Schönborn also refers to the definitive doctrinal statement of the First Vatican Council we've already quoted in a previous chapter: "The same Holy mother Church holds and teaches that God, the source and end of all things, can be known with certainty from the consideration of created things, by the natural power of human reason: ever since the creation of the world, his invisible nature has been clearly perceived in the things that have been made." Obviously, then, he considers the evidence for fine-tuning of the cosmos from the Big Bang forward to be a ripe field from which Catholic scientists, philosophers, and theologians must gather arguments based in the latest science, so that they might use them to build a stronger and stronger case against the notion that the universe is just one big accident. As we've already seen, the attempt to avoid this by the multiverse hypothesis is, if not disingenuous, completely unverifiable. It doesn't stand in the way of further verification of the intricate design of the universe, but rather, by its desperation, attests to the urgency of the atheist-minded to avoid the implications of fine-tuning.

Of course, the Church does not act as a scientist, gathering particular evidence itself, nor is it in the business of dictating the details of research programs. As we've said before, the Church acts not only as a patron of science (hence, the existence of the Vatican Observatory[17]) but also as a general guide and judge in regard to philosophical assumptions and theological implications. In the *Catechism*'s Catechesis on Creation you will not find scientific detail but rather a general doctrinal framework that maintains that the scientific study of origins has "splendidly enriched our knowledge of the age and dimensions of the cosmos" (283); that the "existence of God the Creator can be known with certainty through his works, by the light of human reason" (286); that revelation enriches, rather than contradicts, our understanding of creation known by human reason alone (287); that the glory of God is made manifest in creation (293) clearly showing forth His wisdom and love so we know that "it is not the product of any necessity whatever, nor of blind fate or chance" (295); that God creates from nothing (296) and that creation is evidently well ordered (299); that the God of revelation is not a Deist-type watchmaker god that winds up the world and lets it run on its own, but rather, a God who continually upholds and sustains creation (301); and that creatures are not mere automatons but possess "the dignity of acting on their own, of being causes and principles for each other, and thus cooperating in the accomplishment of his plan" (306).

These are the parameters within which Catholic scientists, philosophers, and theologians may continue to delve into the rich evidence that the entire universe is a grand work of God's wisdom, rather than an unintelligent effect of blind chance and necessity—and that is nowhere clearer than the details of life.

"The Origin of Life Was One Big Happy Accident"

Popular accounts of the rise of life on Earth make it seem as if life's got an easy recipe: mix a few choice chemicals in some primordial ooze, let it simmer for a few million years, stir occasionally with lightning, and soon you've got a batch of living cells champing at their little bits to evolve into fish that, given random variation of their genes and millions of years, will march up the evolutionary slope to become human beings (and, presumably, evolve even further).

This story is, of course, merely a complex variation of the Epicurean tale. One in fact finds the template for all such "scientific" stories about the origin of life and its evolution in the writings of Lucretius.[1] Nothing has changed in the essential story, except the addition of much conjectural scientific detail.

Obviously this story directly contradicts the Church's understanding of creation as purposely wrought by God. To understand this, one does not need to view the beginning of Genesis as a scientific treatise. "It is not the aim of this text," Cardinal Schönborn reminds us, "to give us information as to how this world originated. It is not a text on natural science," and so the "Bible does not offer any theory about the origin of the world and the development of the species."[2] Pope Benedict has said almost exactly the same words.[3] No, the problem with the Epicurean evolution story is not that science tells us that the universe is 13 billion years old, or that life on Earth dates back nearly four billion years. The problem is the "scientific" assertion that it can all be explained as entirely the result of chance and the workings of blind natural laws.

It is a matter of *doctrine* that the rise of life, however it actually occurred in detail, is the result of a purposeful, wise, loving God *and can be known as such*. To quote the *Catechism* again, "Human intelligence is surely already capable of finding a response to the question of origins. The existence of God the Creator can be known with certainty through his works, by the light of human reason, even if this knowledge is often obscured and disfigured by error" (para. 286). The rich evidence about life's origins *should* point to the existence of God, and if it does not, then the problem must be that science has become obscured by error. That is exactly what happened with materialism, and Catholic scientists, philosophers, and theologians must do all that they can to detach the evidence from the deformations caused by ideological materialism. Let's see what we can do to make a good beginning of it.

The Anthropic Universe

We've seen how modern secularism has been trying to put an Epicurean spin on science for a very long time, and it's no different with the question of the origin of life, especially human life: The universe didn't intend us; we are a cosmic accident brewed up on a low-rent planet in an ordinary solar system in a no-account galaxy. Obviously, this story is fashioned against the Genesis account, which, although it doesn't give us scientific detail, makes theologically clear that human beings were purposely, lovingly made by God as the crown and center of His physical creation. Modern science dethroned us . . . so the story goes.

In one sense the story's true. We realize that the Earth is not the physical center of the universe (even though, as we saw in chapter 3, being the center of the universe was not exactly an honor). But what if—strange as it may sound—the more that modern science tried to prove that Earth and human life on it weren't the center of the universe, the more *extra*ordinary we turned out to be? What if our amazing Earth were the center in another way: the center of complex biological life, the center toward which everything is mysteriously bent? What if the human being—*anthrōpos* in Greek—were really, in an essentially scientific way, the culmination of creation? Could such a thing be true?

As it turns out, yes. To understand, we need to go back to material we've covered in the previous chapter. We recall that, going into the 20th century, science wanted to believe that the universe was eternal but discovered that (suspiciously like the creation account in Genesis) the universe had a very definite beginning, "before" which there was neither time, space, matter, nor physical laws. Even more alarming—if you don't want God to exist—this beginning was precisely calibrated in a way that seemed to point to an intelligent cause. But things get even more interesting: scientists began to understand the universe as *anthropic*: that is, the parameters of that calibration seem to have been set for, and culminate in, human beings.

This discovery was, as it were, accidental. Scientists were not looking for it. But when delving into the Big Bang they realized that the precise calibration of laws and fundamental forces wasn't necessary; they just happened to be "just right" for human life.

This brought one Brandon Carter to formulate what came to be called the "anthropic principle." In his words, "What we can expect to observe" as scientists, especially astronomers, physicists, and chemists, "must be restricted by the conditions necessary for our presence as observers."[4] This is a rather paradoxical way of saying that *since* human beings obviously *are* here, since they are intelligent, and since their intelligence has developed to a point where they are capable of advanced science, whatever precise conditions make all that possible did and do, in fact, exist. Otherwise, to steep ourselves in the obvious, we wouldn't be here. *Whatever* conditions, be they the initial conditions of the Big Bang, or those occurring any time during the precise build-up of chemical elements in the first eight billion years of stellar evolution, or finally those exacting conditions that make life *and* science possible on Earth.

To put our argument in condensed form, since human beings are the most complex form of biological life on Earth, the pinnacle of life forms, the only form capable of scientific intelligence, and Earth is the only place that we know with any life at all, science *must* use human beings as the paradigmatic life form defining the parameters of intelligent biological life. We define the very summit of biology and whatever fine-tuning points to biology ultimately points to us. As a theological inference, we are drawn to conclude that the universe was set up for human beings: that is, it was created anthropically.

What that *means* will take us a bit of time to unpack; and indeed, to unpack it, we need to build human beings from the ground (or dust, if you prefer) up. In the next four sections, we'll look at four levels of nature, from lowest to highest, beginning with the chemical foundations, moving on to the origin of the simplest life forms, then the more complex, and finally, we'll look at the most elaborate level of all where we find intelligence—all of which are necessary to "build" a human being. The strange and wonderful thing is that the lowest are built for the highest.

Out of the Dust: The Physical-Chemical Foundation

I hope it is no secret that human bodies are made of chemical elements organized into complex molecules. If it weren't for carbon, hydrogen, oxygen, nitrogen, and a number of other elements, there wouldn't be any life on Earth, let alone human life. To put it another way, human beings share this chemical foundation with the dust beneath their feet or the "stardust," if I might beg a little poetic license, of the most distant star, since the stars are where the elements are cooked up.

But as we've already found out, the presence of a universe existing over a significant amount of time, long enough for stars to cook the chemical elements, is a very precise achievement. Vary the amount of matter at the beginning, and the initial expansion would have been too violent (because of too little matter, and hence too little gravitational mass to overcome the initial impetus) or would have resulted in the universe falling back into itself (too much matter, and hence too much mass, causing a gravitational collapse). Vary the strong or weak nuclear force, and atoms larger than hydrogen couldn't be produced. Fiddle with the nuclear resonance of carbon, and you won't have either carbon or oxygen. Not only is carbon the fundamental biological building block, but oxygen is built from carbon and helium in the furnace of stars. And oxygen, as we all know, is an absolutely necessary element for life, both in itself and as a fundamental constituent of the liquid of life, water.

There we have the first layer of "coincidences," which we discussed in the previous chapter. But then things get even stranger. As it turns out, these fundamental chemical building blocks are *biocentric*; that is, they are artfully contrived for life, as if the initial chemistry of the universe were *made for* the later development of biology. This is an important blow to materialism. Materialism, as part of its inherent antitheistic bent, wants to see biology as an accident of chemistry; therefore, nothing in chemistry should point to biology. But if the universe were made for life by an intelligent cause, we would expect to find that evidence of the plan, the goal, of life on the prebiological level. And that is what scientists have discovered: lifeless matter is tailor-made *for* life, chemistry *for* biology.

The evidence for biocentricism was first presented in scientific detail by Lawrence Henderson in his 1913 classic *The Fitness of the Environment*. Starting out, Henderson did not set out to make a theistic-friendly point. He had been so impressed by Darwin's argument about the survival of the fittest that he wanted to show that not only were the animals that survived the "fittest" but the "actual environment is the fittest possible abode of life."[5] When Henderson looked at the chemical elements and compounds necessary for life, such as carbon and water, he found them not just fit for their task but *supremely fit*.

Science fictionists had been used to spinning out silicon creatures, hydrogen men, and aluminum aliens, as if life could be built up from any old chemical elements, as if one element were as fit as another for making creatures. But the more that science learned about carbon, the actual building block of life, the more they realized that carbon far surpasses any other element as a biological backbone. Carbon is superfit for life, its fitness resting in part on carbon's unmatched ability to form the long "chains" that are necessary to build the complex molecules necessary for life. Carbon is not just a little bit more fit than its only possible chemical competitors—sulfur, tin, silicon, and phosphorous—but maximally fit, leaving the others far back in the cosmic dust.[6]

The same is true for water. Water isn't just one possible liquid of life, marginally superior to other possibilities such as, say, ammonia—it's off the charts spectacular, with a host of what scientists call anomalous properties (properties found only in water or in water to a profoundly higher degree than any other liquid). Subsequent study over the last 100 years has not only confirmed Henderson but extended his analysis far deeper into chemistry and biology.[7]

If we look carefully at all the most basic elements necessary for biology—carbon, hydrogen, oxygen, and nitrogen—we find, in the apt words of Michael Denton that "it is as if from the very moment of creation the biochemistry of life was already preordained in the atomic building process, as if Nature were biased to this end from the beginning."[8]

But here's the problem that Darwinists like Henderson ran into. Darwin tried to explain away God by ascribing the production of species to random variation and survival of the fittest in the competitive struggle of one living thing against another, with the slightly fitter one prevailing. But here we are talking about prebiological superfitness. There is no struggle. There's no randomness. There is no chain of improvement. There's just superfitness for biology *built right into* chemistry. The chemical elements give every indication of having been *made* just for life.

And Then There Was Life . . .

As the secular story goes, the first living cells appeared as a happy accident of chemistry, thanks to chance reactions between chemicals stewing in a prebiotic soup. Lucretius thought it was just that easy, and Darwin thought the process could be duplicated in a "warm little pond, with all sorts of ammonia and phosphoric salts, light, heat, electricity, &c."[9] Such was the thinking of most scientists until, as the 20th century wore on, they discovered how complex the living cell actually was, and so how improbable it would be to produce its integrated components by chance.

This, in and of itself, is an important point, well worth a pause for reflection. According to the warfare thesis, the advance of science is supposed to leave religion behind, knowledge replacing ignorance. As it turns out, quite the opposite has happened. The more science learns about the universe and life, the less plausible simplistic materialist accounts become. Secular stories about the easy chemical creation of life were things of the imagination; the actual complex facts of biology as they have been revealed to us force us to admit that such stories are materialist fantasies. Religion has nothing to fear from the advance of science.

This becomes stunningly clear in regard to Darwinian accounts of the origin of life. You see, for Darwinian evolution to get going, you've got to have something already alive that can replicate and pass on desirable traits. But nothing prior to the cell can do that, and even the simplest cell is itself wondrously complex. Imagine someone thinking that he can drive a car while he's also trying to build it from scratch: the obvious problem is that the car has a certain amount of precisely integrated parts that must already be in place, and be working in conjunction with each other, before it can get anywhere at all. So it is with the cell. In order to "run," it needs a large number of proteins, each made of complex amino acid structures, that provide the framework and working parts of the cell. It also needs the nucleic acids that make up DNA that functions as an information system for its ongoing activity and allows the cell to replicate itself. Both are necessary and both would need to be present for any cell to be minimally functional (actually, it takes a lot more than that to be minimally functional, but we'll give the materialist a little slack for a moment).

The problem is that even the simplest chemical structures of these types are too complex to get by mere random shuffling of chemicals. For example, estimates of the probability of randomly getting one very short strand of amino acids lined up for a modest, functional protein strand run in the neighborhood of a one in 10^{74} chance of hitting the lucky sequence that actually could serve in a cell. (To give you some idea of what this means, you'd be more likely to stumble across a single specially marked atom among all the atoms in the Milky Way galaxy.[10]) And a functioning cell needs a *lot* of distinct proteins—the simplest living cell needs almost 500—and that makes the probability of randomly assembling a suite of proteins for even the simplest cell even more outlandish (something on order of a 1 in $10^{41,000}$ chance).[11] How lucky is that? If, by some magic, I had "hidden" a single atom somewhere, anywhere, in the entire universe and you, by mere chance, happened to find it on the first try—that's actually far, far, far *more* likely than producing the necessary proteins for a functional cell by chance.

If that weren't hard enough, cells are more than the right kind of proteins; they need, *at the same time*, the right sequence of nucleic acids making up their DNA. This creates a chicken-and-egg problem for Darwinists. You need nucleic acids to build the DNA as the informational code to build the right proteins; you need proteins to carry on the activity of the cell according to the code. They must act together as part of an integrally complex process. There's the obvious rub. As historian and philosopher of biology Iris Fry so aptly states, "Proteins and nucleic acids are extremely complex molecules, a fact that makes it hard to imagine their simultaneous synthesis on the primordial Earth. And yet how could the one be produced without the other? This 'chicken-and-egg' problem constitutes one of the major stumbling blocks in research on the origin of life."[12]

All attempts to get around this difficulty by positing a slow building-up of either nucleic acids or proteins have failed—the failures being deeply verified because, happily, scientists have divided themselves into contesting parties, the pro-DNA-ers and the pro-proteinizers, each eagerly showing the defects entailed in the schemes and scenarios of the other.[13] Yet there can't really be a "what's first?" contest. They both have to be there simultaneously, and they must be structurally and integrally related to each other.

Why? Here's an analogy. Pretend that you know nothing about cars. You want to build one blindly; that is, you don't even know what parts you will need. Not having any idea of what cars should be made of, you start randomly shoving together pieces of wood, rubber, stone, glass, plastic, metal—that's what it's like to randomly generate protein chains and nucleic acids. Now suppose that after several billion years of this random process you managed to build up a large stock of real auto parts: wheels, cylinder heads, brake discs, exhaust pipes. How do they go together? And which ones will fit the other ones in just the right way to make a functioning car? Things are even worse than we might imagine. Every single part could fit *except one*, and the car still wouldn't function. The wrong diameter oil filter, or valve sizes that are off by a few millimeters, or wheel bolts that are off by an eighth of an inch, will scuttle the whole project. The fitting-ness of many of the parts is interconnected with the fittingness of other parts. It's not as if you can have a functioning car and then later "evolve" the right wheel bolt size or fuel-air ratio. It all has to work together as a whole from the start, or the car doesn't go. (That's why—as we maddeningly experience—your car may break down or fail to start when even a single part malfunctions.) And since there's no intelligence, there's no method to the trial and error, and every near miss is as good as a mile—coming "close" to randomly assembling a car doesn't make it any more likely you'll get there soon.

So to state the obvious, nothing in the parts themselves will cause them to be chosen or properly fit, and there is no intelligence guiding the choosing. Until the right ones are—by some miracle of chance—put together into a functioning whole, you won't have a car. Such a lucky event is so exceedingly unlikely that giving you a few billion more years wouldn't help.

But when the simplest cells appeared on the Earth some 3.8 billion years ago, it happened very quickly—literally, as soon as the conditions of the cooling Earth would allow them to exist. Viewed from a materialist's viewpoint, this makes no sense. It gives every appearance of being a "setup."

The Miracle of Complex Life on Earth

But we aren't really interested in the simplest cell. We're looking for a cornucopia of life, the astounding biological diversity we find on our Earth. The presence of simple cells, by themselves, doesn't guarantee that we will have all this Edenic splendor. A necessary condition is not a *sufficient* condition, and biological complexity, building upward, requires a whole lot more, even if we just look at the conditions of the Earth itself.

Complex biology needs a rich suite of chemical elements. We've already seen that life cannot occur on just any planet next to any star in any galaxy at any time during the universe's 13-plus billion years. Biological complexity demands chemical complexity, and that means getting a planet with a sufficient array of chemical elements. Given that such elements are the result of billions of years of stellar evolution, and that they are available in sufficient concentration and variety in only a fraction of the universe (in the right part of galaxies of the right type), we can see why the elemental richness of Earth is a rarity rather than a commonplace.

But that's not nearly enough. A livable planet must be just the right distance from just the right kind of star. It must have just the right axial tilt and spin rate and cannot have an erratic orbit that would cause enormous temperature swings. As I mentioned in chapter 5, it must have volcanoes, plate tectonic activity, and a water cycle to keep elements circulating and available for biology. It must have sufficient water, not too little or too much. It must have the right kind of atmosphere with the right amount of oxygen (too little, and there cannot be life; too much, and things continually go up in flames); that atmosphere must also let in visible light for photosynthesis but screen out other, harmful wavelengths on the electromagnetic spectrum that would destroy plant and animal life. The planet must also have a built-in thermostatic system, including clouds, a carbon dioxide and rock weathering cycle, and sufficient surface water to absorb heat and water currents to disperse it.

I have listed only a small percentage of the conditions necessary for a planet to become a living Earth.[14] But the point should be obvious. We live in a "sweet spot," a solar system of just the right kind, on a planet that meets the exacting hierarchy of delicate conditions required for complex life.

We mentioned already that the simplest living cells showed up too quickly for a materialist explanation. But then things went into a long lull. A bit less than two billion more years passed before cells complex enough for significant biology, eukaryotes, arrived on the scene. And then relatively little happened for about another billion and a half years.

So far on the biological timeline we've already "used up" four billion of the Earth's 4.5 billion years—almost 90 percent—with very little to show for it. Unlike the sudden appearance of simple cells, this does fit the materialist theory of origins: according to Darwin, random variation and natural selection should—*must*—work very slowly, at an imperceptibly gradual crawl. The first three billion years of slow development from the simplest cell, then, is just what Darwin (or Epicurus) would have predicted.

Now the rub: if it takes three billion years to get from the simplest cell to a cell fit for complex biology, how long—given the biological distance we still have to climb—should it take to get to, say, an iguana, a turtle, a swan, an ox, or a human being by the very same blind process of random variation and natural selection? We've only got ten percent of our time left. If we had another 500 billion years, things might be different (although there's still the sticky question of why random evolution would climb up in complexity rather than simply spread out in the simplest biological equilibrium). But we don't. The speed of diversification and development, as it actually occurred after the "lull," is more like a biological explosion or frantic bloom. In fact, science says there was an explosion, called the Cambrian Explosion, at about 530 million years, where quite suddenly and without biological precedent (that is, without evidence of evolutionary precursors) all the basic body plans of all modern phyla of animals appeared. From this explosion forward, creatures developed and diversified at an extraordinary pace, leaving in the fossil record traces of their often bizarre life forms' coming and going. From the Cambrian Explosion on, things happen too quickly (at least for

Darwinism), and we begin, rightly, to suspect that the universe and especially the Earth were exceedingly well designed for the development of life. We might even say that evolution works too well for it to be by chance.

This brings us to another problem for materialists. Since Darwin defined evolution by blind processes as necessarily slow and gradual, the fossil record should reflect that gradual change, step by minute step. Instead, it shows creatures stubbornly staying the same for millions of years, and then quite suddenly changing in pronounced, not gradual ways. As far as the fossil record goes, species seem to appear out of nowhere.

The largest leap, in the ascending, unfolding scale of beings is of course the leap to human beings. We are the very apex of biological complexity: an animal in which all the lower levels of being—the nonliving matter of physics and chemistry, the cellular capacities to take in nutrition, grow, and reproduce; the animal powers of sensation, mobility, and judgment—are taken up into a being that can reason and think abstractly, a being who can ask the question, "Where did I come from and what am I made of?"

The Strangest Creature of All: *Homo sapiens*

Wisdom, *sapientia* in Latin, is our defining characteristic. Any theory of human origins that cannot explain this singular characteristic, or even worse, explains it away, is at best useless and at worst pernicious. Any science of human origins that cannot explain the advent of human scientists is no science at all.

As noted in the introduction, the Church stands back from the particular theories in any science offered at any one time, and in the case of human origins, that is very prudent indeed. The science of human origins has been, over the last century and a half, dominated by Darwinians who aim to demonstrate man's evolution from some apelike ancestor in order to strike a blow against the Judeo-Christian understanding of humanity. That goal has defined their assumptions, and the assumptions have guided their search for evidence—what they look for, what they dwell on, and what they ignore. Thus, as with some other sciences, the state of research has been deformed by a materialist bent.

Let me provide a particularly illuminating example. The received assumption, reaching all the way back to Darwin's *Descent of Man*, is that showing *any* commonality between human beings and other animals (especially apes), in regard to physical structure, emotional makeup, or mental capacity, is enough to establish that there is a smooth evolutionary ride up, rather than a qualitative leap, from animals to human beings. So a chimpanzee using a stick to dig out termites, or an orangutan putting a leaf on his head to shield it from sun or rain, is enough to cement the smooth Darwinian connection between ape and man. The point of research, under this view, is obviously to focus intensely on every similarity, no matter how small or general, and to *disregard the qualitative differences as inconsequential.* The result is a scientific methodology that stresses continuity and ignores embarrassing discontinuity.

Because this distortion is so entrenched, I was happily shocked to pick up a recent issue of *Scientific American* and find an article by Marc Hauser, professor of psychology, human evolutionary biology, and organismic and evolutionary biology at Harvard University, saying exactly the same thing—and calling his colleagues to task for ignoring the obvious.[15] In Hauser's words,

> Charles Darwin argued in his 1871 book *The Descent of Man* that the difference between human and nonhuman minds is "one of degree and not of kind." Scholars have long upheld that view, pointing in recent years to genetic evidence showing that we share some ninety-eight percent of our genes with chimpanzees. But if our shared genetic heritage can explain the evolutionary origin of the human mind, then why isn't a chimpanzee writing

this essay, or singing backup for the Rolling Stones or make a soufflé? Indeed, mounting evidence indicates that, in contrast to Darwin's theory of a continuity of mind between humans and other species, a profound gap separates our intellect from the animal kind.[16]

The gap is too profound to ignore any longer, and that means that scientists must change the way that they look at human origins. For Hauser, gathering evidence means gathering *all* the evidence, and that includes the evidence for the profound, qualitative differences between human beings and any other animals. I stress that he was not at all trying to make any theistic point. He was merely urging his colleagues in human evolutionary biology toward an honest and realistic assessment of the evidence and toward future research programs that stressed the enormous differences between the intellectual capacities of human beings and animals.

A chimp may use a stick, but the leap from there to drilling holes in a bone to make a flute is immense, involving a level of abstraction that allows the creation of an instrument that is an extension of the creative mind and not just an extension of the inquiring hand. Under artificial conditions, some animals, such as crows, can use a single item as an instrument to get what they want: for example, bending a piece of wire to use as a kind of hook to fish a desired item out of a glass jar. But human beings combine multiple materials in accordance with detailed knowledge of the constitutive materials and the outside world to create things like telescopes to look at the heavens they desire to know. A leaf hat to a leaf hut may not be much of a leap, but the leap from a leaf hut to a cathedral is, and any account of the origins of human intelligence must provide an explanation for the development of the capacity for both leaps. Although there is obviously communication among animals of the same species, nothing among animals comes close to the abstract, abstruse, multilayered, and complex use of speech by human beings. Certain animals display rudimentary abilities to distinguish small quantities, but no other animals can spin out an intensely detailed string of mathematical equations and puzzle about how they might help explain the order of the universe.

If we looked at our bodies alone, as the materialist would, we might well agree that human beings could have developed, along with chimpanzees, from a common apelike species (species being the least distinct in the taxonomy of biology). But if we looked at our minds alone, we could rightly declare ourselves to have come from an entirely different kingdom (the highest taxonomic difference in biology).

The Difference a Soul Makes

We've now come around to what the Church can say, in most general terms, about the development of human beings. As we noted before, in the encyclical *Humani Generis* (1950), Pope Pius XII excoriated materialism (along with other errors), but said of evolution that "the Teaching Authority of the Church does not forbid that, in conformity with the present state of human sciences and sacred theology, research and discussions, on the part of men experienced in both fields, take place with regard to the doctrine of evolution, in as far as it inquires into the origin of the human body as coming from pre-existent and living matter—for the Catholic faith obliges us to hold that souls are immediately created by God" (para. 36).[17] That last phrase is key, for it is the rational, immaterial soul that makes all the difference, the great qualitative difference in the capacities of the human mind. While physicists, chemists, and evolutionary biologists cannot demonstrate the existence of the soul directly using the particular methods of their sciences, evolutionary biologists demonstrate it indirectly, through its undeniable, measurable effects in creating the enormous qualitative intellectual differences that mark the uniqueness of human beings.

But we would be misrepresenting the Church's position if we gave the impression—to be a bit whimsical—that Catholics should envision an evolutionary scenario where God, brooding over a large group of some rather advanced apes, suddenly drops a couple of rational souls into a promising pair. Discontinuity of mind entails discontinuity of body. Since we are made in the image of God, and are made to be embodied creatures, then our bodies must in some real sense bear forth that image. Being a right handsome ape is not enough. I quote extensively from the *Catechism* to drive this neglected point home.

> The human body shares in the dignity of "the image of God": it is a human body precisely because it is animated by a spiritual soul, and it is the whole human person that is intended to become, in the body of Christ, a temple of the Spirit:
> Man, though made of body and soul, is a unity. Through his very bodily condition he sums up in himself the elements of the material world. Through him they are thus brought to their highest perfection and can raise their voice in praise freely given to the Creator. For this reason man may not despise his bodily life. Rather he is obliged to regard his body as good and to hold it in honor since God has created it and will raise it up on the last day.
> The unity of soul and body is so profound that one has to consider the soul to be the "form" of the body: i.e., it is because of its spiritual soul that the body made of matter becomes a living, human body; spirit and matter, in man, are not two natures united, but rather their union forms a single nature. (paras. 364–65)

Accordingly, the Church forbids us to approach ourselves either as monkeys with really big brains or mere monkeys in whom God happened to have injected immaterial souls—that is, as if there were only a quantitative material difference, and not an essential spiritual and formal difference, or as if there were a formal difference without any corresponding physical difference, between us and the animal kingdom. Unfortunately, there are all too many Catholics, especially scientists, who hold to something like the soul-injected-into-an-ape view of human origins. That is understandable, given that Darwinian-defined approaches to evolution have reigned over the last century and a half, but it is not acceptable.

The ensouled ape view is unacceptable on another level. On the level of revelation, the Incarnation, the union of God and man, makes it doubly important that the flesh of the Word made flesh not be united to just any old animal or even a promising ape. We are made in the image of God and the Word becomes flesh to save and restore that image. In the Incarnation, Jesus Christ restored that image to its pristine condition. Even more (as Cardinal Schönborn, relying on the Church Fathers, has elegantly argued) Jesus in the flesh shines forth directly, through the divinity of the Son, the image of the Father, manifesting an even deeper connection between Jesus Christ's human face and bodily form, and the invisible God.[18]

The Surprising Intelligibility of the Universe

There is something even more amazing about our humanity and our world, something that, if they thought about long and honestly enough, should turn all atheists and agnostics toward belief. It is strange enough to dwell on the enormous leaps in development that make possible the inquiring mind of the scientists, but it is stranger still to realize that the universe is so suspiciously well suited to inquiry. Why should there be such a happy coincidence between our mind and the world? Why should the universe be intelligible? Why should we creatures be able to ply its depths, layer by layer? Why is there any connection whatsoever between the abstract art of mathematics contrived by human beings and the laws and parameters of the universe that were certainly not of our making? If such were not the case, science would be impossible.

This strange "coincidence" has been noted by more and more scientists.[19] It is something that *needs* to be explained because it can hardly be a coincidence—science is too wonderfully effective in too many areas. Just as the original conditions of the universe didn't have to be fine-tuned, so also there is no reason the universe *has* to be intelligible. Its intelligibility itself is one of the things that we must grasp with our intelligence. Pope Benedict held up this all-important connection in his Regensburg Address in 2006, putting it in the proper theological context of the relationship between faith and reason.

> Modern scientific reason quite simply has to accept the rational structure of matter and the correspondence between our spirit and the prevailing rational structures of nature as a given, on which its methodology has to be based. Yet the question why this has to be so is a real question, and one which has to be remanded by the natural sciences to other modes and planes of thought—to philosophy and theology. . . . The West has long been endangered by this aversion to the questions which underlie its rationality, and can only suffer great harm thereby. The courage to engage the whole breadth of reason, and not the denial of its grandeur—this is the program with which a theology grounded in Biblical faith enters into the debates of our time.[20]

For Pope Benedict, science itself points toward the profound connection between the reason—the Word, the *Logos*—of the Creator God and the *logos* of human beings made in His image. This connection is not something accidental. How could an accidentally contrived universe develop deep intelligibility for mathematical reasoning billions of years before there were human beings who developed the ability for abstract mathematical reasoning? Rather, we must follow our reason and recognize that the deep intelligibility of nature is a gift from a wise Creator for creatures made in His image who are therefore capable of science, of coming to know the glory of creation. In this sense, the very existence of science acts as a demonstration of the existence of God.

We've now come to the very pinnacle of anthropism. In human beings, all the elements of material creation are brought up into a glorious thinking creature, the only one of its kind. To repeat the words of the *Catechism*, "Man, though made of body and soul, is a unity. Through his very bodily condition he sums up in himself the elements of the material world. Through him they are thus brought to their highest perfection and can raise their voice in praise freely given to the Creator" (para. 364). Part of our praise comes from our natural feeling of wonder, of awe, at the intricacy of our own biology and all creatures great and small beneath us. This recognition of the deep order of nature is the greatest natural wonder of all—that we can know the universe and that the universe is knowable by such creatures as we are.

Of course, the obvious rejoinder is this: "Well, we may be top dog on Earth, but what about all those aliens?" To questions about extraterrestrial life we now turn.

THE SEVENTH CONFUSION

"The Vastness of the Universe Means Extraterrestrial Life Must Exist"

We just *know* that aliens have to exist, don't we?[1] The universe is billions of miles across and billions of years old. There are billions of galaxies in the universe, billions of stars in each galaxy, and who knows how many billions of planets orbiting these billions of stars. Since we know that life arose and developed on our own planet by random material processes, it is inconceivable that there would not be life somewhere else in the cosmos. In fact, it must be a near certainty that there's life—and not just life, but intelligent life. Real extraterrestrials (ETs) of every imaginable size, shape, and constitution! Therefore, we humans ain't nothing special.

The "ain't nothing special" flourish should let us know that this story goes all the way back to the ancient Epicureans. As we'll see, belief in the inevitability of ETs has very ancient roots. But the Epicureans weren't the only ones convinced of it. A parallel source of speculation came up within Christianity and is still around today. The reasoning goes something like this: God is all-powerful. The universe is really big. There are uncountable stars out there that must have uncountable planets. It is inconceivable that Almighty God would make so grand a universe and not fill every nook and cranny with life of every sort. Since we know He created life abundantly on our planet, He certainly could not have left the universe otherwise empty! Therefore, there must be endless planets out there, whether just like Earth or wildly different from it, and on them, ETs of every imaginable kind manifesting God's endless creative power, wisdom, and goodness.

Note, although both arguments aim for the same conclusion, they do it for opposite reasons: one to put an end to religious belief by taking away our special position in the cosmos and the other to expand religious belief beyond the confines of Earth. But here's the really amazing thing. *We have exactly zero actual scientific evidence that there are aliens.* None. Zilch. Nada. No little green visitors. No text messages from space. No alien corpses or gadgets retrieved by NASA. We've written books about ETs, produced movies about them, conjectured long into the night about them, argued about how they must look and where they must be. But the simple, hard, real scientifically verified truth is that we have *exactly* as much evidence that aliens exist as we do that leprechauns exist. People claim to have seen both, even talked with them, but when you push for any hard facts remaining to verify their experience, it all dissolves into mist.

That's a very important fact that we must keep in mind, and it can't be stressed enough in regard to the effect on faith. Conjecturing about aliens as if they've already been proven to exist, or that their existence is a rational or statistical inevitability, tends either to destroy or distort faith. From the side of the secularists, the certainty that they exist allows them to dismiss the notion that some kind of a divine being created human beings in His image. For if aliens are spilling out of every crack in the universe, then human creation is just one more cosmic accident. From the religious side, the near certainty of intelligent extraterrestrial life forces us to reconstruct central Christian doctrines to make room for ETs in the cosmic Church. Zero evidence seems like a rather shaky starting point for such a project.

We might even say, given what we've covered in the last chapter, that we have less than zero evidence, if we might put it that way, because all the latest scientific evidence points in the other direction: the complex and delicate parameters that make intelligent life possible on Earth are so stringent that the possibility of life existing elsewhere approaches zero. It can't be exactly zero—we know *we're* here—but the more we find out, the more the possibility shrinks to the one actual example, us. So not only do we have zero evidence of actual ETs, we have much evidence that their existence is highly improbable.

If we have no evidence, and a vanishing possibility, then why do we have such a strong, unquenchable belief that ETs must exist? That's a very good question, and we'll need to begin by taking a large step back historically.

Epicurean Atomism and Epicurean Aliens

Christians inclined toward believing in the existence of extraterrestrials should be aware that such belief makes for strange bedfellows. We've already met Democritus, Epicurus, and Lucretius, and we are now aware that their evolutionary argument was undertaken to eliminate religion. Part of that argument was the evolution of extraterrestrial life. It goes like this. Eternal atoms whirling about during infinite time create, quite by accident, an endless plurality of worlds. So it was that, without any actual evidence, Democritus first declared that there are "innumerable worlds."[2] And Epicurus, coming next, asserted confidently that there simply must be "an unlimited number of *cosmoi* [i.e., worlds], and some are similar to this one and some are dissimilar. . . . For atoms of the sort from which a world might come to be or by which it might be made are not exhausted [in the production] of one world or any finite number of them, neither worlds like this one nor worlds unlike them. Consequently, there is no obstacle to the unlimitedness of worlds."[3] And Lucretius, in his *On the*

Nature of the Universe, made bold to assure his readers, "So many atoms, clashing together in so many ways as they are swept along through infinite time by their own weight, have come together in every possible way and realized everything that could be formed by their combinations."[4] He then drew the inference *with* a theological conclusion:

> Granted, then, that empty space extends without limit in every direction and that seeds [i.e., atoms] innumerable in number are rushing on countless courses through an unfathomable universe under the impulse of perpetual motion, *it is in the highest degree unlikely that this Earth and sky is the only one to have been created* and that all those particles of matter outside are accomplishing nothing.
>
> When there is plenty of matter in readiness, when space is available and no cause or circumstance impedes, then surely things must be wrought and effected. You have a store of atoms [in the universe] that could not be counted out by the whole population of living creatures throughout history. You have the same natural force to congregate them in any place [throughout the universe] precisely as they have been congregated here [on Earth]. You are bound therefore to acknowledge that in other regions there are other Earths and various tribes of men and breeds of beasts. . . .
>
> Bear this well in mind, and you will immediately perceive that *nature is free and uncontrolled by proud masters* and runs the universe by herself without the aid of gods.[5]

We must stress the obvious point, given that Democritus, Epicurus, and Lucretius lived over 2,000 years ago, that their speculations could not be based on any scientific evidence, either astronomical (since they didn't have telescopes) or terrestrial (since they had no way to detect whether their hypothetical atoms actually existed, or any evidence that mere atomic jostling ever produced anything). They didn't form their philosophy on scientific facts. Instead, the desire that we be free from the "tyranny" of religious belief led them to imagine a natural philosophy in which multiple worlds with multiple kinds of intelligent life were produced by chance.

So we've found one very important reason why at least certain kinds of people want aliens to exist: the same old desire that drives scientific materialism in other areas—the desire to kill God, leaving nature, and especially human beings, "free and uncontrolled by proud masters."

What about the Early Christians?

We are already aware, from our discussion in the chapter on Darwinism and evolution, that Christians adamantly rejected Epicureanism, and that would include especially the notion that mere random natural processes could create the world, let alone a plurality of inhabited worlds.

Beyond a severe dislike of Epicureanism, there were both cosmological and theological reasons why early Christians either did not believe in extraterrestrials or refused to speculate about them. The early Christians held to a geocentric universe: the Earth was the place where all heavy, material things collect, and thus the only location possible for intelligent *embodied* beings. Everything above the Earth must be inhabited by something unearthly and unearthy (i.e., immaterial or ethereal). Nor did Christians have any need to invent alien life to keep them company. According to Scripture, the universe out there is already quite well populated with intelligent extraterrestrials of every imaginable grade and rank—they're called Angels.

But far more important for the first Christians, human beings were the center of the cosmic drama of redemption. The

Incarnation was the union of God's divinity with our humanity, and we were made, body and soul, in the image of God. The Church's source of revelation went directly back to Jesus Christ Himself and His apostles. This tradition did not include any notion of the redemption of other intelligent, embodied creatures that existed elsewhere, nor any hint, from Jesus, that other worlds existed to which He was likewise wedded by other modes of incarnation to save other sinful races.

For all these reasons, we find no evidence of speculation about extraterrestrials among the early Christians. Not only did such speculation run directly against the central doctrinal claims of Christianity but it also smacked of Epicureanism (which entailed, among the other things we've mentioned, the denial of the immortal, immaterial soul, Heaven, and Hell). Small wonder the early Christians tossed the Epicurean package, extraterrestrials and all, into the abyss of doctrinal errors. And there it stayed for nearly a thousand years.

The Middle Ages and Extraterrestrial Speculation

Here is where things get tricky. What caused the rise of ET speculation in the Middle Ages is, at first blush (and even second blush), rather obscure. It arose accidentally, so to speak, as a reaction to what is called radical Aristotelianism, and to understand what happened will take a bit of explaining.

Beginning about AD 1100, text after text of the great Greek philosopher Aristotle reached the West, and Christians were suddenly confronted with a unified, well constructed account of the universe, an account written by a pagan for pagans. Importantly, Aristotle denied that there could be a plurality of worlds, even though he argued for the eternality of the world.[6] His was the cosmology that, united with Ptolemy, provided the medievals with their understanding of the cosmos. As we've noted, the notion of Earth's centrality on the Aristotelian-Ptolemaic view was rooted in Earth's "grossness," that is, the fact that the Earth was where all the heavy stuff in the universe gathered, and so again, there could only be one physical world and one place where embodied life could be found.

Although we commonly read in history textbooks that everyone in the medieval Church cheerfully accepted Aristotle, the situation was much more complex. There were actually three reactions to Aristotle's purely natural, non-Christian philosophical account: vehement rejection (the radical Augustinians), careful embrace (St. Thomas), and passionate embrace (the radical Aristotelians, principally, Siger of Brabant). Those who passionately embraced Aristotle tended to look down their noses at mere theologians, and regarded Aristotle's texts as the real font of wisdom compared with the trickle one could find in the Bible. Around 1265 a conflict between the two radical wings began to heat up, resulting in the famous (or, for Thomists, infamous) 219 Propositions in 1277, issued by the bishop of Paris, Etienne Tempier, one proposition of which condemned all those who hold the Aristotelian position that the first cause cannot make more than one world.

It should be stressed that the aim of Bishops Tempier's condemnation was *not* to affirm a plurality of worlds but to affirm God's omnipotence against any account of nature that seemed to restrict God's powers. Aristotle's insistence that there could only be one world accorded nicely with the Genesis account of creation, but it appeared to the radical Augustinians that it made God the servant of natural necessity rather than its master. The remedy, so Bishop Tempier and his followers thought, was to assert that the first cause could indeed create a plurality of worlds (even if we know *by revelation* that He happened to make only one).

But the condemnation had an unforeseen effect. No sooner had the ink soaked into the vellum than speculation among Christians about a plurality of worlds began in earnest. By the beginning of the 15th century, that speculation had led some

Christian thinkers to affirm the existence of extraterrestrial life. In his *On Learned Ignorance* (1440), Nicholas of Cusa argued,

> Life, as it exists on Earth in the form of men, animals and plants, is to be found, let us suppose, in a higher form in the solar and stellar regions. Rather than think that so many stars and parts of the heavens are uninhabited and that this Earth of ours alone is peopled—and that with beings, perhaps of an inferior type—we will suppose that in every region there are inhabitants, differing in nature by rank and all owing their origin to God, who is the centre and circumference of all stellar regions.[7]

And then Nicholas goes on to offer an admirably contrived zoology, even while admitting it is all entirely speculative.

> Of the inhabitants then of worlds other than our own we can know still less, having no standards by which to appraise them. It may be conjectured that in the area of the sun there exist solar beings, bright and enlightened denizens, and by nature more spiritual than such as may inhabit the moon—who are possibly lunatics—whilst those on Earth are more gross and material. . . . And we may make parallel surmise of other stellar areas that none of them lack inhabitants, as being each, like the world we live in, a particular area of one universe which contains as many such areas as there are uncountable stars.[8]

So it was that Christian speculation about lunatics and solarians moved from the lunatic fringe closer to the acceptable center. But what is such supposing and conjecturing based on? Evidence? Revelation? Reason? No. In fact, it issued from an unhappy union of sloppy logic and untethered imagination. To affirm God's omnipotence (by condemning the proposition that "the first cause cannot make more than one world") does not entail that God actually *had* to create multiple worlds (and, moreover, people them with hosts of aliens). As for footloose imagination, the embarrassing claim about solarians and lunatics speaks for itself. The title "learned ignorance" takes on new meaning, since such wild and sure speculations were possible only because of the complete ignorance of the actual conditions on the sun and moon coupled with nearly complete ignorance of what is biologically and chemically possible.

It did not take long before speculation seeped into dogma. About 30 years after the appearance of Nicholas of Cusa's *On Learned Ignorance*, a French theologian, William Vorilong, in the midst of a speculative reverie about another world, assured his readers that "if it be inquired whether men exist on that [other speculative] world, and whether they have sinned as Adam sinned, I answer no, for they would not exist in sin and did not spring from Adam . . . As to the question whether Christ by dying on this Earth could redeem the inhabitants of another world, I answer that he is able to do this even if the worlds were infinite, but it would not be fitting for Him to go unto another world that he must die again."[9]

Speculation in the Early Modern World

As the medieval world transformed into the modern, the resurgence of Democritan-Epicurean-Lucretian atomism combined with the steady stream of Christian ET ruminations led to an ever-stronger stream of ET speculations—or we might say a double stream, since the pagan stream weaved in and out of the Christian stream, sometimes using the certainty of ETs to attack Christianity and sometimes going with the flow of Christian speculation to flood and dilute Christian dogma from within.

We find the passion for aliens in the heretical Giordano Bruno's

On the Infinite Universe and Worlds (1584), and since Bruno was an advocate of both Epicurean atomism and Copernicanism (for his own purposes), Epicurean speculation about ETs and Copernicus's uprooting of the Earth seemed to go together, making the latter suspect by association with the former. The great astronomer Johannes Kepler (1571–1630) thought life on Jupiter and on our moon was probable. Galileo, already swimming in heated water, was reserved, but one of his great advocates and a disciple of Bruno's as well, Tommaso Campanella (1568–1634), had no such qualms. Campanella, whose orthodoxy was quite suspect, wrote an apology for Galileo even before he was arrested, defending him and the necessity of ETs in the Copernican-Galilean system. The Anglican divine John Wilkins published a work anonymously with one of those long, lovely titles typical of the 17th century, *The Discovery of a World in the Moone, or, A Discourse Tending to Prove That 'Tis Probable There May Be Another Habitable World in That Planet* (1638). Here again, Copernicanism and ETism were entwined—just five years after Galileo's trial, mind you—the first taken to lead ineluctably to the existence of the second. Wilkins's book was immensely popular and influential. Seeing that the spirit of speculation was loosed on Europe, we are not surprised that one of the first works of science fiction appeared that same year, Bishop Godwin's *The Man in the Moone, or a Discourse of a Voyage Thither.*

We find further endorsements of the inevitability of ETs by the Cambridge Platonist Henry More (1646), the French scientist Pierre Borel (1657), and perhaps most famously and influentially by Bernard le Bovier de Fontenelle in his *Conversations on the Plurality of Worlds* (1686). Although Isaac Newton avoided the issue (at least publicly), his disciples did not, first among them Rev. Richard Bentley who in his Boyle Lectures of 1692 declared that the heavenly bodies must have been "formed for the sake of Intelligent Minds," asking rhetorically, "why may not all other

Planets be created . . . for their own Inhabitants which have Life and Understanding?"[10] Why not, indeed?

The floodgates of modern ET speculation were wide open by the end of the 17th century, just as ancient Epicurean atomism was given new life by being taken up into a modern form of materialism; and so the atomists' belief in extraterrestrials blossomed anew with the advance of the materialistic view of modern science that was being championed both by the secular-minded and by some Christians. In contrast to the ancient antagonism between such materialism and Christianity, modern materialistic atomism met with Christian theologians moonstruck by the possibility of lunatics. With great irony, the Epicurean-Lucretian cosmology, designed to eliminate religion, was now welcomed as the bearer of galactic Good News.

Runaway speculation on ETs marked the century of science initiated by Galileo and triumphantly sealed by Newton. Our analysis would be incomplete, however, if it did not include the *visible* support that the plurality-of-worlds theory seemed to receive with the invention of the telescope. When in the early 17th century the new "spyglass" (as Galileo called it) was trained on the heavens, they were found to be far deeper and more populated with stars than anyone could ever have imagined. Were these not the infinite suns illuminating the infinite worlds promised by Epicurus and Lucretius? Or speaking from the opposite vantage point of Christianity, how great is the creative power of God! Surely, He would not have made all those millions of suns for no reason! Surely, revolving around them were planets teeming with life. The conclusion seemed irresistible. The advance of the Copernican-Galilean system among scientists also aided the cause because Galileo's spyglass revealed that the moon, and by implication, the planets, had rough and earthy surfaces. So Aristotle was wrong: the heavenly bodies were not made of some ethereal element; therefore embodied existence was possible on them.

The Later Modern Era of Speculation
(and Secularization)

From approximately 1700 to 1900, there was a rising flood of scientific-philosophical-theological speculation on the nature of extraterrestrial life. From this period we can cull a veritable bestiary of extraterrestrials that were supposed to inhabit every known planet in our solar system, as well as the sun and moon and, beyond that, every star, planet, and comet in the universe.

Such speculation often came from poets swept away by the new science, such as Richard Blackmore who in his epic poem *Creation* (1712) confidently declared that "We may pronounce each orb sustains a race/Of living things, adapted to the place," or the more famous Alexander Pope, whose *Essay on Man* (1733–34) spoke of "other planets [that] circle other suns" where "vary'd Being peoples ev'ry star."[11] Later, William Wordsworth waxed poetic about "the red-haired race in Mars" and the "Towns in Saturn," certain that "worlds unthought of" by previous ages remained undiscovered "till the searching mind/Of Science laid them open to mankind"[12]—a hint that the Christian religion was (still) ignorant of the greatest truths that only science could reveal.

Soon the poets turned against Christianity more directly, using the certain knowledge of other inhabited planets as a foil against faith. In an explanation of his *Queen Mab* (1813), Percy Bysshe Shelley declared that, given the plurality of other worldly inhabitants, it is "impossible to believe that the Spirit that pervades this infinite machine begat a son upon the body of a Jewish woman," and furthermore, "All that miserable tale of the Devil, and Eve, and an Intercessor, with the childish mummeries of the God of the Jews, is irreconcilable with the knowledge of the stars."[13]

Nor were philosophers immune from the fever. Immanuel Kant declared in his *Universal Natural History and Theory of the Heavens* (1755) that it was impossible for an infinite God in an infinite universe to allow all that space to go unpopulated, therefore "the cosmic space will be enlivened with worlds without number and without end." Kant believed that the planets of our solar system were peopled with a gradation of intelligent life from the sun outward, with Earth occupying the center of intellectual ability between the lunkheaded Mercurians and Venusians and the superminds on Jupiter and Saturn. Accordingly, Kant surmised that Mercurians and Venusians were too stupid to sin, and Jovians and Saturnians too smart; so with the possible exception of Martians, Earth was the only planet needing a Saviour.[14] The positivist philosopher Auguste Comte, who (we recall) was certain that science was allowing us to leave behind the age of religion and superstition, declared magnanimously that if Mercury, Venus, and Jupiter were inhabited, "we can regard those inhabitants as being in some fashion our fellow citizens," but lamented that "the inhabitants of other solar systems will be complete strangers."[15]

But ET reverie was not the sole province of the poets and philosophers. The best scientists of the day made their contributions as well. Sir William Herschel (1730–1822), the astronomer who discovered Uranus in 1781, claimed that he saw near-certain evidence of forests, circular buildings, canals, roads, and pyramids on the moon—all, of course, signs of a brimming lunatic population. He was equally certain that the known planets of our solar system were all peopled, and insisted the sun was filled with solarians "whose organs are adapted to the peculiar circumstances of that vast globe."[16] Johann Bode (1747–1826), a director of the Berlin Observatory and famous for Bode's Law, asked of these same solarians, "Who would doubt their existence?" His reason for such certainty was quasi-theological. "The most wise author of the world assigns an insect lodging on a grain of sand and will certainly not permit . . . the great ball of the sun to be empty of creatures and still less of rational inhabitants who are ready gratefully to praise the author of life."[17] The same reasoning led him to affirm the existence of extraterrestrials on the moon, Mercury, and Venus.

We find, throughout this period, similar speculations approved by equally eminent scientists: Sir William Rowan Hamilton (1805–56), Sir Humphry Davy (1778–1829), Sir David Brewster (1781–1868), François Arago (1786–1853), Hans Christian Oersted (1777–1851), Richard Owen (1804–72), J. Norman Lockyer (1836–1920), Jean Liagre (1815–92), Jules Janssen (1824–1907), William Pickering (1858–1938)—and the list goes on well into the 20th century, a *who's who* of the leading astronomers and other scientists. As François Plisson, a French physician and cool-headed critic of extraterrestrial mania, wrote in 1847, "Almost all the astronomers of our day, and the most eminent among them, freely adopt the opinions that not long ago were viewed as being able to spring only from the mind of a madman."[18]

If belief in solarians, lunatics, Jovians, Venusians, Mercurians, and Martians seems madness now, during the 18th and 19th centuries it was taken to be the only rational, scientifically grounded view. Small wonder, then, that theologians—both Christian and Deist—felt not only inspired but obliged to incorporate extraterrestrials into their systems. Looking first at the Christian attempts, one notices immediately that the doctrine of the Incarnation underwent a transformation, as well-intentioned Christians rushed to keep up with the latest menagerie of extraterrestrials. We've already mentioned the Reverend John Wilkins's *Discovery of a World in the Moone* and Bishop Godwin's *The Man in the Moone.* A bit later, and pushing things a bit further, *Traité de l'Infini Créé* (*Treatise on the Created Infinite*) was published in 1769, allegedly by Abbé Malebranche but actually by Abbé Jean Terrasson. In it, Terrasson argued that the Incarnation was *not* peculiar to our planet. If "it is asked . . . if the eternal Word can unite himself hypostatically to a number of men [i.e., different rational creatures on multiple planets], one responds without hesitation—yes. The men would all be men-God [*hommes-Dieu*], men in the plural,

God in the singular, because these men-God would in effect be several in number as to human nature, but they would be only one in respect to divine nature."[19] Indeed, even where there was no Fall, Christ would embody Himself as a member of the race, for they deserved this honor even more than those who had fallen.

Other attempts to reconcile Christian revelation with extraterrestrials abound. William Hay (1695–1755) argued for multiple modes of salvation entailing multiple modes of Christ's Incarnation; James Beattie (1735–1803) asserted that Christ's Incarnation, death, and Resurrection served as an inspiring example for all extraterrestrials; and Beilby Porteus (1731–1808) maintained that the Incarnation actually extends to *all* extraterrestrials. By the beginning of the 19th century, belief in the plurality of worlds was so well accepted, especially among Protestants, that it was now incorporated as an essential element of evangelical orthodoxy. Some proponents, such as Thomas Chalmers (1780–1847), were fairly cautious. But others showed less restraint.

To such "orthodox" speculations, we should add those of the influential visionary Baron Emanuel Swedenborg (1688–1772), who claimed to have conversations with the Angels of each of the planets of our solar system and reported that all the planets are actually inhabited by human souls of those who died on Earth. It was he who informed us matter-of-factly that lunarians speak very loudly "from the abdomen" because "the Moon is not surrounded with an atmosphere of the same kind as that of other Earths."[20] Later Swedenborgian offshoots were just as daring, such as the former Baptist Thomas Lake Harris, who declared (in 1850) that he too had visited the heavens, and was shown that inhabitants of the "star" Cassiopeia "feed chiefly upon the aromas of exquisite flowers," while Mercury is peopled with a bevy of "Christian Platonic Philosophers." Harris also discovered that Earthlings are the only fallen race.[21] Ellen Harmon (1827–1915), prophetess and foundress of the Seventh-Day Adventists, reported after one of her visions that "the inhabitants [of Jupiter] are a tall, majestic people, so unlike the inhabitants of Earth. Sin has never entered here."[22]

The Mormons, founded by Joseph Smith, were another sect inspired by astronomical speculation; they also believed in a universe populated by a plurality of gods, Angels, and extraterrestrials. Smith took his revelatory cues from Moroni, an angelic being, who supposedly revealed the basics of Mormonism on a set of gold plates, which Smith later transcribed into *The Book of Mormon* (1830). It was not in this book, but in other Mormon writings, *The Doctrine and Covenants* (1835) and *The Pearl of Great Price* (1851), that a plurality of inhabited worlds was set forth. The interesting aspect of this pluralism is that gods are now included as fellow inhabitants among the hierarchy of beings scattered throughout the cosmos. As Parley Pratt, Mormon theologian, declared, "Gods, angels and men, are all of the same species, one race, one great family widely diffused among the planetary systems, as colonies, kingdoms, nations, etc."[23] Mormonism, with all the bizarre cosmic speculation in its core theological dogmas, represents the inevitable and ultimate result of the attempts at syncretism by Christians with ET mania. As we see, doctrine becomes entirely defined, or better, entirely redefined, according to the particular fancies of charismatic leaders who claim newly revealed astronomical "truths" that supersede biblical truths. Even God becomes an ET, while ETs become gods.

Whereas Christians and heretical spin-offs tried to fit Jesus Christ into the new cosmic scheme, some Deists understood the clear implications of a plurality of worlds for the specific claims of the Christian Incarnation. Thomas Paine's anti-Christian *Age of Reason* (1794–1807) is an important case in point. Perhaps more clearly than anyone else of the time, the Deist Thomas Paine realized that the existence of a multitude of inhabitable worlds (and, thus, of extraterrestrials) was entirely incompatible with Christianity: "To believe that God created a plurality of worlds at least as numerous as what we call stars, renders the

Christian system of faith at once little and ridiculous and scatters it in the mind like feathers in the air." For those who attempted a reconciliation of such plurality with Christianity, Paine warned that "he who thinks that he believes in both has thought but little of either."[24] Paine, convinced of plurality, chose Deism.

This last is an important point. Deism rejected the Incarnation and with it most if not all of revealed theology. At the same time, well-intentioned Christians, wanting to keep up with the latest science, chiseled away at the doctrine of the Incarnation to make it fit such pluralism, while other Christians, bent on saving Christianity from irrelevance, likewise hacked away at the embarrassing particularity of the Incarnation until the doctrine itself became largely irrelevant. Orthodoxy was battered from both sides by those absolutely convinced, beyond doubt, of the existence of Jovians, Saturnarians, Venusians, Martians, solarians, and lunatics. Since all of this tended to erode the Incarnation, the effect of incorporating aliens was to transform Christianity into Deism.

As the 19th century wore on, the latent secularism in Deism surfaced as atheism and orthodoxy was battered by yet another foe in the name of science. Although Darwin himself apparently didn't enter the fray, and his bulldog advocate Thomas Huxley displayed only cautious optimism, the Epicurean-Lucretian foundations of Darwinism soon became handy scientific sources for the belief that godless evolution must be taking place on innumerable planets. Atheism no longer needed the halfway house of Deism. Secularization could now proceed at full throttle. And the belief in extraterrestrials was an essential part of the new materialist creed, just as it had been an essential part of the old one.

One of the important sources of criticism against endless ET speculation came from William Whewell, whose essay *Of the Plurality of Worlds* (1853) criticized the ungrounded optimism of alien enthusiasts. Whewell was one of the first modern scientists to look carefully at the actual conditions that make life on Earth possible and so one of the first to realize that those conditions do not, and cannot, pertain on the other planets in our solar system (let alone on the moon or sun). Whewell is, we might say, the father of the anthropic principle. He also realized, just as clearly as Thomas Paine had, that ungrounded speculation about a plurality of inhabited worlds was irreconcilable with Christianity.[25]

Although Whewell had reasons as a Christian to defend Christianity against ungrounded ET speculation, he attacked cosmic pluralism on the basis of science, on the basis of what could really be counted as physically, chemically, and biologically possible on the other planets in our solar system, the moon, and the sun. That's what gave his book the stinging force that elicited so many spirited responses. But even as advances in chemistry and astronomy vindicated Whewell, there were still many prominent 19th-century scientists who continued to assert that even life on our sun was still possible, including the English chemist Thomas Lamb Phipson, the English astrophysicist J. Norman Lockyer, founder and first editor of the prestigious scientific journal *Nature*, and astronomer and mathematician Jean Baptiste Joseph Liagre. And we should not forget the eminent scientist John William Draper, whom we met in chapter 1 as the author of *History of the Conflict between Religion and Science*. Unsurprisingly, Draper was an ET enthusiast, taking the necessary existence of multiple worlds as evidence of the foolishness of Christianity's provincial claims.

The 20th Century: The Evidence of Absence

Only by the beginning of the 20th century was science advanced enough to move from speculation to the actual search for hard evidence. One of the greatest hopes for alien enthusiasts was that, with the discovery and advance of radio technology, we could pick up signals from space. The first to express such hopes was the American physicist and engineer Nikola Tesla, who in 1901 thought he'd gotten such a signal. Notions of the possibility of other signals along the electromagnetic spectrum being sent to Earth percolated in the rest of the first half of the 20th century. In 1959 physicists Giuseppe Cocconi and Philip Morrison published a paper in the prestigious science journal *Nature* titled "Searching for Interstellar Communications," and this jump-started the search in the second half of the century. Soon enough, the biggest, most expensive equipment in the most up-to-date astronomical observatories was being bent to space, listening intently for even a whisper from ETs. By the 1970s and 1980s SETI (Search for Extra Terrestrial Intelligence) projects were running full steam, the most famous being the SETI Institute founded in 1984.[26] The stated mission of SETI is "to explore, understand and explain the origin, nature and prevalence of life in the universe."[27] The only problem—millions and millions of dollars later—is that they haven't detected any.

As amply documented by Steven Dick in *Life on Other Worlds: The 20th-Century Extraterrestrial Life Debate*, by the end of the 20th century, scientists had demonstrated to all but the most zealously intransigent that—humble Earth excepted—our solar system was devoid of intelligent life and most likely devoid of *any* life (except the faintest of evidence for microbial life on Mars). And endless hours of scanning the sky for signals from beyond our solar system hasn't netted anything but lifeless static.

Yet the dismal result of the high-tech search for extraterrestrials only stirred advocates all the more, resulting in the optimistic but defensive battle cry: "The absence of evidence is not evidence of absence." While this might warm the dwindling fires in the enthusiasts' hearts, it pays little service to reason. To be blunt, since the absence of evidence was the negative result of a century-long search for aliens, the absence of evidence *is* evidence for absence. What else would it be?

A naysayer might ask, "But if what you're saying is true, doesn't the lack of scientific evidence for angels prove that angels don't exist?" Such a riposte merely deflects attention from the seriousness of the self-inflicted wound. Again, whether or not Angels exist, scientists *were* actively looking for extraterrestrials, convinced without a shred of evidence that they must exist. The simple truth remains: over the span of the 20th century, science systematically eliminated the possibility of extraterrestrials in our solar system, and their existence elsewhere has dwindled from an absolute necessity to a dim chance. Further, those who compare Angels to aliens forget that Angels are by definition immaterial beings. What kind of a scientific test would one devise to locate a being who, because it is not embodied, has no location? Extraterrestrials, on the other hand, are *supposed to be* material organisms. If they really had been flitting around and about Earth, we should have been able to detect them the same way we detect any other physical body.

If we might end with a bit of a jab: for the nonbeliever already convinced that Angels don't exist, to be forced to admit that he has no more reason to believe in aliens than in Angels, is an admission of defeat. This admission is all the more important precisely because extraterrestrials seem to function for secularists as material substitutes for Angels.[28] In the great religion of secularism, aliens have now been reduced, at best, to a matter of faith.

Lessons for Theology

The Catholic Church does not have an official position about extraterrestrial life. But the necessity of safeguarding a whole set of central doctrines in regard to the Incarnation of Jesus Christ and the creation and nature of human beings make it clear that speculation is not welcome. And the notion that we need to make way in our theology for those inevitable aliens when they visit us is even less welcome. As the *Catechism* states, "Christ, the Son of God made man, is the Father's one, perfect, and unsurpassable

Word. In him he has said everything; there will be no other word than this one" (para. 65), and so what was revealed about the Word united to human flesh is definitive, and no mention of multiple incarnations is made in either Scripture or Tradition. "Christian faith cannot accept 'revelations' that claim to surpass or correct the Revelation of which Christ is the fulfillment" (para. 67). The addition of multiple incarnations would be, to say the least, a significant correction. Moreover, human beings on Earth, not multiple forms of alleged intelligent life living elsewhere, are the aim of creation: "The universe, created in and by the eternal Word, the 'image of the invisible God,' is destined for and addressed to man, himself created in the 'image of God' and called to a personal relationship with God" (para. 299). "*Man is the summit* of the Creator's work" (para. 341), not just one more intelligent, embodied life form, and the Incarnation, where "the Son of God assumed a human nature in order to accomplish our salvation" (para. 461), is a "unique and altogether singular event" (para. 464) not just another instance in a potentially infinite series. Nor, in all this, should we overlook the effect of alien speculation on Marian dogma. If there were multiple incarnations, wouldn't there be multiple mothers of God?

Unfortunately, several prominent Catholics—such as Guy Consolmagno, S.J.; Monsignor Corrado Balducci; and Fr. José Gabriel Funes, the pope's astronomer at the Vatican Observatory—have spoken out favorably about ETs, even though we have no evidence for their existence, and they have even taken up questions (in the speculative spirit we've already found in the 18th and 19th centuries) about alien sin and salvation.

And what has the Vatican's position been? In 2009, the Vatican's Pontifical Academy of Sciences hosted a five-day conference on astrobiology. Father Funes, who headed up the conference, had already made clear where he stood on the issue in a famous interview with *L'Osservatore Romano* titled "The Alien is My Brother," stating that the existence of ETs "is possible, even if until now, we have no proof. But certainly in such a big universe this hypothesis cannot be excluded."[29] Apparently Father Funes shares the notion that God wouldn't leave such a big universe empty. And in the same spirit as the flurry of Christological speculation in the 18th and 19th centuries, Fr. Funes sees the obvious need to offer his own theological ruminations about the status of alien souls: "We could think that in this universe there can be 100 sheep, equivalent to different kinds of creatures. We, belonging to human kind could be precisely the lost sheep, the sinners that need the shepherd. God became man in Jesus to save us. In that way, assuming that there would be other intelligent beings, we could not say that they need redemption. They could have remained in full friendship with the Creator." Then how are they related to salvation history? "Jesus became man once and for all. The Incarnation is a single and unique event. So I am sure that also they, in some way, would have the chance to enjoy God's mercy, just as it has happened with us human beings."[30]

How to understand this? Does the Vatican now approve of ET speculation? We must clear up some all-too-inviting confusions. First, the head of the Vatican Observatory does not speak in the name of the Church or the pope. These thoughts are his own. The Magisterium has not spoken directly on the matter.

Secondly, there is a difference between what we can say on the basis of science and what we must say as the basis of faith. The existence of ETs cannot be entirely ruled out by science. What science can do, and has done, is decrease the likelihood that ETs exist by showing in ever more detail the layers upon layers of delicate conditions that must pertain for complex biological life to exist. A conference on astrobiology, if it truly followed the flow of evidence rather than speculative ardor for ETs, would focus on the increase in our scientific understanding of these delicate conditions and hence the increasingly rare possibility of the existence of other Earthlike planets. The advance of science over the last 25 years demonstrates the decreasing possibility of alien life;

therefore it should lead us to speculate about it less, not more.

Third, and perhaps most humbling for those inclined to hitch theological doctrines to the science of the day, the history of science should give us sufficient warning against unwarranted theological speculation based on transient scientific "certainties." Think how foolish we would appear today if the Catholic Church had modified its doctrine of redemption to make room for solarians, Venusians, Mercurians, Martians, and lunatics? We would be in the same speculative boat as Swedenborgians, Seventh-Day Adventists, and Mormons. The lesson? There's nothing more dated than the ideas of those who insist on keeping their ideas up-to-date. The best remedy for theologians inclined to speculation is a long, deep draught of the elixir of the history of science, where it becomes evident that today's verities are often tomorrow's absurdities.

Next, Catholics should be wary of leaning on revived forms of the sloppy logic of omnipotence, which arose after the publication of Tempier's 219 Propositions in 1277. In its original form, it is a theological truism: "God is omnipotent; therefore God can create anything." But all too soon, this became a very different proposition: "Since it is possible for God to create anything, then God *must create everything possible*; therefore, extraterrestrials *must* exist, and the doctrine of the Incarnation *must* be expanded accordingly." This triple inference not only is invalid but leads to foolishness. Would we say that since God is all-powerful, He *must* create leprechauns, become incarnated as a leprechaun, and also redeem their fallen race?

Finally, Catholics should be equally wary of the idea that God would somehow be a second-rate deity if He allowed human beings to be the only intelligent embodied beings in the universe since that would mean a lot of wasted space. What frightens us into making such claims is, I believe, the immensity of space itself. But while the vastness of the universe rightly humbles us, its size means nothing to God, an immaterial intelligence. Since He has no size, it is all the same to Him whether He makes the universe as big as a pin or a pin as big as the universe. Moreover, even on scientific grounds, bigness does not imply anything about some kind of necessary biological fullness. The Big Bang means that the universe has to be as big as it is and as old as it is for even one form of intelligent life, human life, to have had sufficient time to develop—the expansion of space and the passing of time are inextricably intertwined. That is, the stellar evolution of elements taking place as the universe expands is necessary for the creation of sufficient elements for biological complexity and the eventual "home" to put them in. Thus according to the physical laws God created, the universe had to be as big as it is for just one planet, Earth, to exist as a habitable planet.

A related point: Catholics should not be cowed by the materialist's logic of probability, which had its birth in Epicurus and Lucretius. The logic runs thus: our sun is a star; since the number of stars is so vast, sheer probability demands that there must be other inhabited planets beyond our solar system. But for a Catholic, probability does not demand any such thing, unless we think (with Epicurus) that the universe is governed by chance—and *that*, of course, would be a reason to give up our Christianity. The creation of Earth is not a matter of chance, so it is not governed by questions of probability.

I can already hear the parting objection: "But what would you do if extraterrestrials actually showed up? It is *possible*, after all. And the Church hasn't pronounced one way or the other." I am as prepared for the arrival of extraterrestrials as I am for that of leprechauns and for the same reason: all evidence points to their nonexistence, and yet it remains a very, very remote possibility—so remote that to change our central doctrines to accommodate either possibility would be folly.

Moreover, the notion that aliens out there would be visiting us any time soon (or in fact, already have visited us) is a scientific absurdity. The nearest star to us is Proxima Centauri, more than four light-years away. No matter what you've seen on *Star Trek*, no creature is going to travel at the speed of light and make a short four-year trip of it. Somehow these guys would have to travel 25,222,492,800,000 miles. Our spaceships can go a bit over 17,000 miles per hour. At that speed, it would take about 1,483,676,047 hours or 169,253 years to travel from Proxima Centauri to Earth! How many generations of aliens would have to be on the ship for it to finally dock at Earth? What do they eat all that time? How do they refuel? Why wouldn't their spaceship simply wear out? Do they have the equivalent of little NAPA parts-delivery shuttles (complete with the signature plastic NAPA hat) bringing them replacement parts along the way?

There are a host of other problems, both obvious and arcane, with such an alien jaunt, especially if we try to understand it purely on secular terms, which I'll append to this chapter. Enough has been said already to make it clear that we have no scientifically compelling reasons to believe in the existence of ETs. In fact, the advance of science actually points toward greater and greater skepticism. So again, faith has nothing to fear from the advance of science—unless, of course, it is faith in aliens.

APPENDIX

More Evidence against a Visit by Aliens

First of all, Proxima Centauri is not a fit "sun" for life, so the aliens are going to have to come from further out. Perhaps it's the next furthest star out? Say, alpha Centauri B? But if we are considering things from the secular angle, the probability that life just *happens* to have evolved by chance so close, given the billions and billions of other stars and galaxies, is beyond belief, like finding that two needles in a haystack the size of Texas just happen to exist side by side.

Second, said aliens would already have to have developed technological capabilities far beyond anything we have today to make the trip practicable, and done it about a couple hundred thousand years earlier. But life on Earth developed about as fast as is possible, with the simplest cells popping up as soon as the Earth cooled sufficiently. The development of complex life was made possible only by the strangest of events, the Big Bang of biology, the Cambrian explosion. Why would another planet experience these fortuitous events? Moreover, our advanced technological development did not have to happen, but depended on a long string of contingencies—after all, it developed only in the West and depended on the choices, actions, fortunate discoveries, genius, and perseverance of particular persons. There didn't *have* to be a Newton, a Lavoisier, a Maxwell, an Einstein, and so on—and we are not listing the names of those less famous who were so integral to the long development of the various supporting practical sciences that allow technology, such as metallurgy, mechanics, and the other industrial sciences.

Third, we're talking about real travel, possible forms of travel. It's all very well for science fiction to imagine that aliens have somehow figured out how to travel at the speed of light, or to take short-cuts through worm holes, or by some other fantastic way to cut out years or miles from their alleged journey, but just as with speculations about Jovians or solarians, such things are not based upon real knowledge of the limits of speed, material, and biology. Think you can push a button and (like the guys in *Star Trek* or *Star Wars*) jump to light speed? Then you should do a little research on the effects of g-force on the human body— jumps in acceleration of such magnitude would simply crush an alien body flat.

Fourth, since travel takes so long and there are so many stars to choose from, why would aliens choose *here*, of all places, for a visit? Alien enthusiasts assume a kind of strange importance to Earth, so much so that extraterrestrials (ETs) seem to buzz around humble Earth like moths around a light bulb. If we think ETs simply *must* exist out there somewhere, and we realize that, on scientific grounds alone, intelligent alien life would be exceedingly rare, then exactly why would these alleged aliens choose our solar system out of the billions, upon billions, upon billions of other possibilities?

The upshot is this: even if against all real possibility we allow ourselves to assume that there is intelligent life out there, and we stick to scientific facts rather than invoke scientific fantasies, aliens would never in a billion, billion years visit us. So we are doubly excused from having to worry about ETs: the possibility that they exist is next to zero, and the possibility that they would visit Earth is the smallest fraction of that.

CONCLUSION

In his General Audience of March 24, 2010, Pope Benedict spoke on the patron saint of scientists, St. Albert the Great—great in his own right and great as the teacher of St. Thomas Aquinas.

> Above all, St Albert shows that there is no opposition between faith and science, despite certain episodes of misunderstanding that have been recorded in history. A man of faith and prayer, as was St Albert the Great, can serenely foster the study of the natural sciences and progress in knowledge of the micro- and macrocosm, discovering the laws proper to the subject, since all this contributes to fostering thirst for and love of God. The Bible speaks to us of creation as of the first language through which God who is supreme intelligence, who is the Logos reveals to us something of himself. The Book of Wisdom, for example, says that the phenomena of nature, endowed with greatness and beauty, is like the works of an artist through which, by analogy, we may know the Author of creation (cf. Wis. 13:5). . . . How many scientists, in fact, in the wake of St Albert the Great, have carried on their research inspired by wonder at and gratitude for a world which, to their eyes as scholars and believers, appeared and appears as the good work of a wise and loving Creator! Scientific study is then transformed into a hymn of praise.[1]

Much more could be said about the relationship of the Church to science, but here we have the very heart of it. Science, true science, cannot contradict the Faith; rather, it can only enrich it, giving us a deeper and deeper understanding of God's magnificent wisdom as manifest through his created works.

Yet as we have seen, science is human; that is, human beings, with all their faults, foibles, confusions, and errors are the ones carrying out the work of science. It does not occur in some kind of pure, theoretical vacuum, but is the result of human intellectual and physical effort. As the history of science reveals, the search for truth is often bent or distorted by bad philosophy, principally materialism, that restricts human reason and hence human science to the assumption that only material reality and material causes exist. In such a restricted view, the activity of science itself ceases to make sense, for if materialists were right, then the human mind and its thoughts would simply be effects of aimless material causes. Yet the capacity to discover truth is only possible if we assume a spiritual, intellectual power in human beings that is not subject to the laws and physical processes it discovers. This spiritual power is, in fact, proven by the very fact that science exists. We cannot have a view of science into which science itself cannot fit.

The Church's guard against philosophical distortion is an essential part of its mission, and as I hope the reader now understands, the real source of most of the conflict that the Church has experienced in relationship to particular scientists or sciences. The Church is not antiscience (as the warfare myth would have it) but antimaterialist. Of course, that does not mean the Church itself falls into some kind of Gnostic heresy, denying the physical aspects of being, even and especially human beings, and treating the material world or the human body as inconsequential or inessential. We are a true union of body and soul, material and immaterial elements, and so our science necessarily partakes of the capacity to know as defined by this union. Unlike the angels, we use both our intellect and senses to know, and so our science is a union of theory and experiment, sudden illumination and empirical testing, hypotheses and laborious searching with our own eyes for verification. As long as we keep in mind these essential spiritual and material elements of science, then we won't, as scientists, define our capacity to know as if it were purely immaterial or reality as if it were only material.

In guarding both aspects of reality, the Church actually fosters a new approach to science, one that goes beyond the centuries-long domination of materialist paradigms, making use of all the rich store of knowledge that scientists have gathered under the inadequate materialist view, and stretching it beyond its reductionist limitations to take in a much more comprehensive scientific understanding of reality—pushing a half-truth to the whole truth. When we stop viewing plants, animals, and human beings as reducible to mere chemical aggregations, as accidents of physical-chemical laws, then we will find that the order of being actually ascends from the smallest parts of matter through a hierarchy of inanimate wonders that are well-designed as the foundation for living creatures, these creatures themselves running from the simplest cells to the most complex animals, and ultimately to the one animal endowed with an intellect, an immaterial soul, capable of science. The material finds its culmination in the spiritual, as human beings sum up in themselves all that is below them, and become the one spiritual-material creature capable of knowing itself, its world, and through these, its creator. In this culmination the love of science and the love of God unite.

Revelation transcends even this knowledge, but in transcending, it does not destroy it. Grace builds upon nature, the supernatural upon the natural. And that means, once again, that science cannot contradict the Faith.

What we need, it seems to me, is a shaking of foundations, a waking-up from a centuries-long materialist slumber. Reading, study, reflection, and prayer will have to precede the future task of restructuring modern science to take into account its legitimate insights but remove the groundless biases and distortions. What might we read to give us a jolt—so that a deeper, more comprehensive understanding of science can emerge?

Well, I think it is best to admit up front that I can offer no authoritative list, but only pass on what books seem to me, as a matter of my own experience, to be most helpful.

First, I would strongly urge a close reading of the *Catechism of the Catholic Church*. The *Catechism* gives Catholics the widest possible authoritative framework for our seeking the natural foundations of truth in creation (including its proper moral and social parameters), not only for its own sake but in light of our revealed eternal destiny.

As the footnotes to the previous chapters indicate, I've found several books to be especially illuminating in regard to a new approach to science that focuses on what is peculiar about human life and its exacting conditions, especially about what allows us to be scientific creatures. The best of these books are Peter Ward and Donald Brownlee, *Rare Earth: Why Complex Life is Uncommon in the Universe* (New York: Copernicus, 2000), Guillermo Gonzalez and Jay Richards, *The Privileged Planet: How Our Place in the Cosmos Is Designed for Discovery* (Washington, DC: Regnery, 2004), and Michael Denton, *Nature's Destiny: How the Laws of Biology Reveal Purpose in the Universe* (New York: Free Press, 1998). Although I don't agree with everything said in them, they open up a new and immensely important and fruitful way for scientists to carry on their work. It was on the basis of these that I wrote my own contribution, with Jonathan Witt, *A Meaningful World: How the Arts and Sciences Reveal the Genius of Nature* (Downers Grove, IL: IVP, 2006). Each of these books has an extensive, and far more technical bibliography.

Of course, I don't mean to exclude any number of other wonderful works written by scientists, historians, philosophers, and theologians, both Catholic and non-Catholic. I've read so many, and these are only a fraction of what is out there. But we all find those handful of books that really make a difference in the way we see certain subjects, and I believe it is best to recommend a smaller number than a larger, since the larger the stack, the more burdened the prospective reader feels looking at it, and so, no beginning is made at all.

Notes

Introduction

1. G. K. Chesterton, *Orthodoxy* (New York: Doubleday, 1959), 100–101.

2. J. L. Heilbron, *The Sun in the Church: Cathedrals as Solar Observatories* (Cambridge, MA: Harvard University Press, 1999), 3.

3. See Neil Baldwin, *Edison: Inventing the Century* (Chicago: University of Chicago Press, 2001), especially chapter 10. First of all, he was not the first to work on the problem of electric luminescence. Humphry Davy (1778–1829) seems to have been the first, and a long list of partially successful inventors and scientists follow leading up to Edison's triumph in 1879. Edison himself had his own personal struggles in life before becoming an inventor, including being considered a bit slow in school and also gradually losing his hearing from an early age. In regard to the problem of creating a viable electric light, the main difficulty was figuring out what the glowing filament should be made of, and it cost Edison more than a lot of sweat. He fell ill with "neuralgia," he accidentally burned the side of his face (which caused his eyes to water constantly), and in the midst of his labors, his wife went into labor. On top of all this, Edison, a bit of a showman, had "announced" prematurely to the public that he was on the cusp of victory, and so he was constantly badgered by reporters about his too-slow progress.

Chapter 1

1. For an up-to-date assessment of Draper's thesis and its long reverberation down through a seemingly endless number of textbooks and popular science books, see Ronald Numbers, ed., *Galileo Goes to Jail, and Other Myths about Science and Religion* (Cambridge, MA: Harvard University Press, 2009). See also David Lindberg and Ronald Numbers, eds., *God and Nature: Historical Essays on the Encounter between Christianity and Science* (Berkeley, CA: University of California Press, 1986), introduction; and Lindberg and Numbers, "Beyond War and Peace: A Reappraisal of the Encounter between Christianity and Science," *Perspectives on Science and Christian Faith* 39, no. 3: 140–49. (Happily, this last essay is also available on the web at *http://www.asa3.org/ASA/PSCF/1987/PSCF9-87Lindberg.html*.)

2. From the introduction to Andrew Dickson White, *A History of the Warfare of Science with Theology in Christendom* (New York: Appleton, 1896). White's book is available on the web at http://englishatheist.org/white/contents.html. White had published a shorter, earlier version of his two volume argument in 1876, entitled, more economically, *The Warfare of Science*.

3. There are few screeds against the Church as lively and literary as Part IV of Hobbes's *Leviathan* (1651), titled "Of the Kingdom of Darkness."

4. Henri Thierry Baron d'Holbach, *The System of Nature*, vol. I (Middlesex, England: The Echo Library, 2006), 7.

5. Baron d'Holbach, *The System of Nature*, vol. 1, 10.

6. John Paul II, *Fides et Ratio* (Boston, MA: Pauline Books, 1998), p. 7.

7. John Paul II, *Fides et Ratio* (Boston, MA: Pauline Books, 1998), Chapter V, Section 49, pp. 66–67.

8. John Paul II, *Fides et Ratio*, Chapter V, Section 50, p. 67.

9. John Paul II, *Fides et Ratio*, Chapter V, Sections 52–56, pp. 68–76.

10. Noah Efron, "That Christianity Gave Birth to Modern Science," in Ronald Numbers, ed., *Galileo Goes To Jail, and Other Myths about Science and Religion*, p. 79.

11. Alfred North Whitehead, *Science and the Modern World* (New York: Macmillan, 1967), 12. Whitehead's book was originally published in 1925.

12. For up-to-date accounts, see John Hedley Brooke, ed., *Science and Religion: Some Historical Perspectives* (Cambridge: Cambridge University Press, 1991); David Lindberg, *The Beginnings of Western Science: The European Scientific Tradition in Philosophical, Religious, and Institutional Context, Prehistory to A.D. 1450* (Chicago: University of Chicago Press, 1992); Edward Grant, *The Foundations of Modern Science in the Middle Ages: Their Religious, Institutional and Intellectual Contexts* (Cambridge: Cambridge University Press, 1996); Gary Ferngren, *Science and Religion: A Historical Introduction* (Baltimore, MD: Johns Hopkins University Press, 2002); and James Hannam, *God's Philosophers: How the Medieval World Laid the Foundations of Modern Science* (London: Icon, 2009); as well as Numbers, *Galileo Goes to Jail*; and Lindberg and Numbers, *God and Nature*.

13. As an introduction see Syed Nomanul Haq, "That Medieval Islamic Culture Was Inhospitable to Science," in Ronald Numbers, ed., *Galileo Goes To Jail*, chapter 4; for more detailed analyses see George Saliba, *Islamic Science and the Making of the European Renaissance* (Cambridge, MA: MIT Press, 2007); Mark Graham, *How Islam Created the Modern World* (Beltsville, MD: Amana Publications, 2006); and Jonathan Lyons, *The House of Wisdom: How the Arabs Transformed Western Civilization* (New York: Bloomsbury Press, 2009).

14. See my *Moral Darwinism: How We Became Hedonists* (Downers Grove, IL: InterVarsity Press, 2002); Peter Gay, *The Enlightenment, An Interpretation: The Rise of Modern Paganism* (New York: Norton, 1966); Catherine Wilson, *Epicureanism at the Origins of Modernity* (Oxford: Oxford University Press, 2008); and Jonathan

Israel, *Radical Enlightenment: Philosophy and the Making of Modernity, 1650–1750* (Oxford: Oxford University Press, 2001).

15. See Charles Webster, *From Paracelsus to Newton: Magic and the Making of Modern Science* (Cambridge: Cambridge University Press, 1982); William Eamon, *Science and the Secrets of Nature* (Princeton: Princeton University Press, 1996); D. P. Walker, *Spiritual and Demonic Magic: From Ficino to Campanella* (London: University of London, 1958); Frances Yates, *Giordano Bruno and the Hermetic Tradition* (Chicago: University of Chicago Press, 1964).

16. On the connections in regard to alchemy and chemistry see my *Mystery of the Periodic Table* (Bathgate, ND: Bethlehem Books, 2003), which is an introduction to the history of chemistry for young people, but is quite serviceable as a general introduction; and on a more sophisticated level, my *Meaningful World: How the Arts and Sciences Reveal the Genius of Nature* (Downers Grove, IL: InterVarsity Press, 2006), especially chapter 5; John Read, *From Alchemy to Chemistry* (New York: Dover, 1995; originally published in 1957); Cathy Cobb and Harold Goldwhite, *Creations of Fire: Chemistry's Lively History form Alchemy to the Atomic Age* (New York: Plenum Press, 1995).

17. See Hannam, *God's Philosophers,* chap. 15.

Chapter 2

1. For those interested, there are a number of fine sources on the Internet that give a solid introduction to Near Eastern mythology, for example, http://home.comcast.net/~chris.s /assyrbabyl-faq.html, http://www.sacred-texts.com/ane/index .htm. For more detailed information, see Stephanie Dalley, *Myths from Mesopotamia: Creation, the Flood, Gilgamesh, and Others* (Oxford: Oxford University Press, 2009); and Samuel Kramer, *The Sumeri-*

ans: Their History, Culture, and Character (Chicago, IL: University of Chicago Press, 1971).

2. For an excellent scholarly overview, see Annette Yoshiko Reed, "Was There Science in Ancient Judaism? Historical and Cross-cultural Reflections on 'Religion' and 'Science,'" *Studies in Religion* 36, nos. 3–4 (2007): 461–95. Accessed November 8, 2010, http://sir.sagepub.com/cgi/content/abstract/36/3-4/461.

3. *Book of Enoch* 72:1, accessed November 2010, http://www .sacred-texts.com/bib/boe/index.htm.

4. For an important example of Judaism as an exception, see the fifth-century AD midrashic compilation *Genesis Rabbah*. Reed, "Was There Science in Ancient Judaism?" 473.

5. St. Thomas Aquinas, *Summa Theologiae*, IIaIIae Q. 95, a. 1, *sed contra* and reply to objection 1.

6. St. Thomas Aquinas, *Summa Theologiae*, IIaIIae Q. 95, a. 6. Fathers of the English Dominican Province translation, Vol. III (New York: Benziger, 1981).

7. Michael Shank, "That the Medieval Christian Church Suppressed the Growth of Science," in *Galileo Goes To Jail, and Other Myths about Science and Religion*, ed. Ronald Numbers, 21–22. For more information on the founding and curriculum of the universities see David Knowles, *The Evolution of Medieval Thought*, 2nd ed. (London: Longman, 1988), especially chapters 13–14.

8. Shank, "That the Medieval Christian Church Suppressed the Growth of Science," 26–27.

9. James Hannam, *God's Philosophers: How the Medieval World Laid the Foundations of Modern Science* (London: Icon, 2009), 35.

10. See Lesley B. Cormack, "That Medieval Christians Taught That the Earth Was Flat," in *Galileo Goes To Jail, and Other Myths about Science and Religion*, ed. Ronald Numbers, chap. 3.

11. Hannam, *God's Philosophers*, 37.

12. Quoted in Hannam, *God's Philosophers*, 3.5

13. Hannam, *God's Philosophers*, 270.

14. C. S. Lewis, *The Discarded Image: An Introduction to Medieval and Renaissance Literature* (Cambridge: Cambridge University Press, 1967), 97–98. I was alerted to this through Hannam, *God's Philosophers*, 270.

15. Hannam, *God's Philosophers*, 37.

16. Hannam, *God's Philosophers*, 38.

17. On Richard of Wallingford, see Hannam, *God's Philosophers*, chap. 10.

Chapter 3

1. Stephen Hawking, "Galileo and the Birth of Modern Science," *Invention and Technology* (Spring 2009): 33–34, 36–37 (quote from 36). Available online at http://www.medici.org/sites/default/files/GalileoandtheBirth0ofModernScience.pdf.

2. Dennis Danielson, "The Great Copernican Cliché," *American Journal of Physics.* 69, no. 10 (October 2001): 1029–35; quotes from 1029–30.

3. Thomas Kuhn, *The Copernican Revolution: Planetary Astronomy in the Development of Western Thought* (New York: Vintage, 1957), 169.

4. Danielson, "Great Copernican Cliché," 1031.

5. Galileo Galilei, *The Starry Messenger*, in *Discoveries and Opinions of Galileo*, Stillman Drake (New York: Doubleday, 1957), 45.

6. Danielson, "Great Copernican Cliché," 1032.

7. Danielson, "Great Copernican Cliché," 1033–34.

8. Quotes from Luther, Melanchthon, and Calvin in Kuhn, *The Copernican Revolution*, 191–92.

9. James Hannam, *God's Philosophers*, 316–17.

10. See Thomas Aquinas's commentary on Boethius's *De Trinitate*, called *The Division and Methods of the Sciences* in Armand Maurer's excellent translation with extremely helpful notes (Toronto: Pontifical Institute of Medieval Studies, 1986).

11. Happily, the official statements are available online at http://www1.umn.edu/ships/galileo/library/1616docs.htm.

12. Hannam, *God's Philosophers*, 318.

13. Quoted in Maurice Finocchiaro, "That Galileo Was Imprisoned and Tortured for Advocating Copernicanism," in *Galileo Goes to Jail, and Other Myths about Science and Religion*, ed. Ronald Numbers, 72.

14. For a quick overview see Maurice Finocchiaro, "Galileo Was Imprisoned," 73–74.

15. Galileo Galilei, *The Assayer*, in *Discoveries and Opinions of Galileo*, ed. Stillman Drake, 229–80, quote from 274.

16. I have dealt with Epicurus and Lucretius in much more detail in my *Moral Darwinism: How We Became Hedonists* (Downers Grove, IL: IVP, 2002), especially chapters 1–2.

17. *Moral Darwinism*, chapter 4.

18. *Moral Darwinism*, esp. 41–43.

19. Pietro Redondi, *Galileo Heretic*, trans. Raymond Rosenthal (Princeton, NJ: Princeton University Press, 1987).

20. Offered in the appendix to Redondi, *Galileo Heretic*, 333–35.

21. See especially Redondi, *Galileo Heretic*, chapter 8.

22. We now know, for example, that our solar system is actually between the spiral arms of the Milky Way Galaxy, which is, interestingly enough, the biocentric "sweet spot," distant enough from the center to avoid the ill effects of heavy radiation and the perturbing effects of nearby stars.

Chapter 4

1. Charles Darwin, *On the Origin of Species by Means of Natural Selection, or the Preservation of Favoured Races in the Struggle for Life* (London: John Murray, 1859), Introduction, 5 (Facsimile of the First Edition, Cambridge: Harvard University Press, 1964).

2. Richard Dawkins, *The Blind Watchmaker: Why the Evidence*

of Evolution Reveals a Universe without Design (New York: Norton, 1996), 5.

3. Dawkins, *Blind Watchmaker*, 6.

4. Dawkins, *Blind Watchmaker*, 1.

5. Lucretius, *On the Nature of the Universe*, trans. R. E. Latham (New York: Penguin, 1994), Book 5, lines 418–30.

6. Lucretius, *On the Nature of the Universe*, Book 5, lines 798–800, 837–49, 855–60, 870–79.

7. On the importance of Epicurus and Lucretius in early modernity and the dissemination of their thought throughout Europe see my *Moral Darwinism*, especially chapters 4–6, along with George Hadzsits, *Lucretius and His Influence* (New York: Cooper Square, 1963); Howard Jones, *The Epicurean Tradition* (New York: Routledge, 1989); Peter Gay, *The Enlightenment, An Interpretation: The Rise of Modern Paganism* (New York: Norton, 1977); Margaret Osler, *Atoms, Pneuma, and Tranquillity: Epicurean and Stoic Themes in European Thought* (Cambridge: Cambridge University Press, 2005); and Catherine Wilson, *Epicureanism at the Origins of Modernity* (Oxford: Oxford University Press, 2008).

8. The documents of the council are available online at http://www.ewtn.com/library/COUNCILS/V1.HTM#4. Accessed 8 November, 2010.

9. As declared in the Canons, "If anyone denies the one true God, creator and lord of things visible and invisible: let him be anathema" (1.1); "If anyone is so bold as to assert that there exists nothing besides matter: let him be anathema" (1.2); "If anyone says that the one, true God, our creator and lord, cannot be known with certainty from the things that have been made, by the natural light of human reason: let him be anathema" (2.1); "If anyone says that human studies [including the various sciences] are to be treated with such a degree of liberty that their assertions may be maintained as true even when they are opposed to divine revelation, and that they may not be forbidden by the Church: let him be anathema" (4.2).

10. See my *Moral Darwinism* and more recently my biographical account of Darwin and his theory, *The Darwin Myth* (Washington, DC: Regnery, 2009).

11. For a more detailed account of Darwin's life upon which I rely here, see my *The Darwin Myth*.

12. Alfred Russel Wallace, "Sir Charles Lyell on Geological Climates and the Origin of Species," *Quarterly Review* (April 1869), Vol. 126:359–94; quote from p. 391.

13. Available in Michael Flannery, ed., *Alfred Russel Wallace's Theory of Intelligent Evolution* (Riesel, TX: Erasmus Press, 2008).

14. For a more thorough account, see my *Darwin Myth*, chapters 5–6.

15. Charles Darwin, *The Descent of Man, and Selection in Relation to Sex* (Princeton, NJ: Princeton University Press, 1981), 168.

16. Charles Darwin, *Descent of Man*, 169.

17. Darwin, *Descent of Man*, 162–63.

18. Darwin, *Descent of Man*, 201.

19. Again, see my *Darwin Myth*.

20. Technically, he also added sexual selection to try to explain those traits that didn't seem able to be explained by natural selection, but that addition has nothing to do with the moral outcome of his theory.

21. Section 5 warns, "If anyone examines the state of affairs outside the Christian fold, he will easily discover the principal trends that not a few learned men are following. Some imprudently and indiscreetly hold that evolution, which has not been fully proved even in the domain of natural sciences, explains the origin of all this, and audaciously support the monistic and pantheistic opinion that the world is in continual evolution. Communists gladly subscribed to this opinion so that, when the souls of men have been deprived of every idea of a personal God, they may the more efficaciously defend and propagate their dialectical materialism." Section 6 continues: "Such fictitious tenets of evolution which repudiate all that is absolute, firm and

immutable, have paved the way for the new erroneous philosophy which, rivaling idealism, immanentism and pragmatism, has assumed the name of existentialism, since it concerns itself only with existence of individual things and neglects all consideration of their immutable essences." The encyclical is available online at various places such as http://www.papalencyclicals.net/Pius12/P12HUMAN.HTM.

22. Available online at several places, including http://www.boston-catholic-journal.com/inaugural_address_of_Pope_Benedict_XVI.htm. Accessed November 8, 2010.

23. Pope Benedict XVI, *Spe Salvi*, Section 5, available online at http://www.vatican.va/holy_father/benedict_xvi/encyclicals/documents/hf_ben-xvi_enc_20071130_spe-salvi_en.html.

24. Pope Benedict XVI, *Questions and Answers* (Huntington, IN: Our Sunday Visitor, 2008), 146. The original came from *Meeting of the Holy Father Benedict XVI with the Clergy Of The Dioceses of Belluno-Feltre and Treviso*, Church of St. Justin Martyr, Auronzo di Cadore Tuesday, July 24, 2007, available at http://www.vatican.va/holy_father/benedict_xvi/speeches/2007/july/documents/hf_ben-xvi_spe_20070724_clero-cadore_en.html.

25. Joseph Cardinal Ratzinger, *"In the Beginning . . .": A Catholic Understanding of the Story of Creation and the Fall* (Grand Rapids, MI: Eerdmans, 1995), 50.

26. Christoph Cardinal Schönborn, *"Fides, Ratio, Scientia:* The Debate about Evolution," in *Creation and Evolution: A Conference with Pope Benedict XVI in Castel Gondolfo*, 92.

27. Available online at http://www.nytimes.com/2005/07/07/opinion/07schonborn.html.

28. Christoph Cardinal Schönborn, *Chance or Purpose? Creation, Evolution, and a Rational Faith* (San Francisco, CA: Ignatius, 2007).

29. Simon Conway Morris, *Life's Solution: Inevitable Humans in a Lonely Universe* (Cambridge: Cambridge University Press, 2003).

Chapter 5

1. Epicurus, "Letter to Herodotus," in *The Epicurus Reader*, ed. Brad Inwood and L. P. Gerson (Indianapolis, IN: Hackett, 1994), 6–7.

2. Lucretius, *On the Nature of the Universe*, Book One, lines 52–64, 79–102, 145–58.

3. Isaac Newton, *Opticks* (New York: Dover, 1952), 400.

4. Newton, *Opticks*, 402.

5. John North, *The Norton History of Astronomy and Cosmology* (New York: Norton, 1995), 526.

6. As quoted in Paul Davies, *The Accidental Universe* (Cambridge: Cambridge University Press, 1982), 118.

7. For an overview see Stephen Barr, *Modern Physics and Ancient Faith* (Notre Dame, IN: University of Notre Dame Press, 2003), chap. 15; and Robin Collins, "Evidence for Fine-Tuning," in *God and Design: The teleological argument and modern science*, ed. Neil Manson (New York: Routledge, 2003), chap. 9.

8. Quoted in Gerald Schroeder, *The Science of God* (New York: Broadway, 1997), 5.

9. In addition to what I've just noted, there are any of a number of good books that make available more scientific detail about cosmic fine-tuning. On the exceedingly dense end of things is John Barrow and Frank Tipler, *The Anthropic Cosmological Principle* (Oxford: Oxford University Press, 1986). On a more popular level, there is Martin Rees, *Just Six Numbers: the Deep Forces that Shape the Universe* (New York: Basic Books, 2000); and Paul Davies, *Cosmic Jackpot: Why Our Universe is Just Right for Life* (Boston: Houghton Mifflin, 2007). For an understanding of immense implications of fine-tuning reaching all the way from astronomy to biology see Benjamin Wiker and Jonathan Witt, *A Meaningful World: How the Arts and Sciences Reveal the Genius of Nature* (Downers Grove, IL: IVP, 2006), Guillermo Gonzalez

and Jay Richards, *The Privileged Planet: How Our Place in the Cosmos Is Designed for Discovery* (Washington, DC: Regnery, 2004); Michael Denton, *Nature's Destiny: How the Laws of Biology Reveal Purpose in the Universe* (New York: Free Press, 1998), and John Barrow, ed., *Fitness of the Cosmos for Life: Biochemistry and Fine-Tuning* (Cambridge: Cambridge University Press, 2008).

10. For the latest overview of the entire debate, see Bernard Carr, ed., *Universe or Multiverse?* (Cambridge: Cambridge University Press, 2007). For a critique, see Rodney Holder, *God, the Multiverse, and Everything: Modern Cosmology and the Argument from Design* (Aldershot, UK: Ashgate Publishing, 2004). See also the relevant section of Robin Collins's essay, "The Teleological Argument: An Exploration of the Fine-Tuning of the Universe," in William Lane Craig and J. P. Moreland, ed., *The Blackwell Companion to Natural Theology* (Malden, MA: Wiley-Blackwell, 2009), chap. 4; and the forthcoming Bruce Gordon, "Balloons on a String: A Critique of Multiverse Cosmology," in *The Nature of Nature: Examining the Role of Naturalism in Science,* ed. Bruce Gordon and William Dembski (Wilmington, DE: ISI Books, 2010), chap. 26. My thanks to Jay Richards for bibliographical guidance.

11. See Guillermo Gonzalez, David Brownlee, and Peter Ward, "Refuges for Life in a Hostile Universe," in *Scientific American* 285, no. 4 (October 2001): 60–67. Accessed November 8, 2010, http://atropos.as.arizona.edu/aiz/teaching/a204/etlife/SciAm01.pdf.

12. On the just-rightness necessary for both the sun and the Earth, see Peter Ward and Donald Brownlee, *Rare Earth: Why Complex Life is Uncommon in the Universe* (New York: Copernicus, 2000); and Gonzalez and Jay Richards, *The Privileged Planet* (noted previously).

13. Pope Pius XII, Address to the Pontifical Academy of Sciences, November 22, 1951; reprinted as "Modern Science and the Existence of God," *The Catholic Mind* 49 (March 1972): 182–92.

14. Christoph Cardinal Schönborn, *Chance or Purpose? Creation,*

Evolution, and a Rational Faith (San Francisco, CA: Ignatius, 2007) 37–38.

15. Christoph Cardinal Schönborn, *Chance or Purpose?*, 41. Thirring's *Cosmic Impressions: Traces of God in the Laws of Nature* (Philadelphia: Templeton, 2007) was originally published in German in 2004.

16. Christoph Cardinal Schönborn, *Chance or Purpose?*, 44. *Catechism*, paragraph 286.

17. Visit its website at http://vaticanobservatory.org/.

Chapter 6

1. Lucretius, *On the Nature of the Universe*, Book Five.

2. Christoph Cardinal Schönborn, *Chance or Purpose?*, 55–56.

3. Joseph Cardinal Ratzinger, *"In the Beginning . . .": A Catholic Understanding of the Story of Creation and the Fall* (Grand Rapids, MI: Eerdmans, 1995), "First Homily: God the Creator."

4. See Brandon Carter, "Large Number Coincidences and the Anthropic Principle in Cosmology," in M. S. Longair, ed., *Confrontation of Cosmological Theories with Observational Data* (Dordrecht: Reidel, 1974), 291–98.

5. Lawrence Henderson, *The Fitness of the Environment: An Inquiry into the Biological Significance of the Properties of Matter* (Boston: Beacon Press, 1958, 1913), preface (pages unnumbered).

6. See the immensely illuminating chapter on the super-fitness of carbon in Michael Denton, *Nature's Destiny: How the Laws of Biology Reveal Purpose in the Universe* (New York: Free Press, 1998), chap. 5.

7. For a much more detailed account see my *A Meaningful World*, chapter 7, Michael Denton, *Nature's Destiny*, chapters 2, 4–5, and again, John Barrow, ed., *Fitness of the Cosmos for Life: Biochemistry and Fine-Tuning*. The properties of water have been found so unimaginably extraordinary that there is even a website dedicated

to listing and explaining them, even while scientists continue to add newly discovered anomalous properties, Accessed November 8, 2010, http://www1.lsbu.ac.uk/water/anmlies.html.

8. Michael Denton, *Nature's Destiny: How the Laws of Biology Reveal Purpose in the Universe* (New York: Free Press, 1998), 109.

9. Darwin's famous "warm little pond" rumination can be found in Francis Darwin, *The Life and Letters of Charles Darwin*, 3 vols. (New York: Johnson Reprint Corporation, 1969), vol. 3, 18.

10. See Stephen Myer, *Signature in the Cell: DNA and the Evidence for Intelligent Design* (New York: Harper One, 2009), 211.

11. Myer, *Signature in the Cell*, 213.

12. Iris Fry, *The Emergence of Life on Earth: A Historical and Scientific Overview* (New Brunswick, NJ: Rutgers University Press, 2000), 100.

13. See my *Meaningful World*, chap. 8

14. See Peter Ward and Donald Brownlee, *Rare Earth: Why Complex Life is Uncommon in the Universe* (New York: Copernicus, 2000), Michael Denton, *Nature's Destiny: How the Laws of Biology Reveal Purpose in the Universe* (New York: Free Press, 1998), and Guillermo Gonzalez and Jay Richards, *The Privileged Planet: How Our Place in the Cosmos Is Designed for Discovery* (Washington, DC: Regnery, 2004).

15. Marc Hauser, "Origin of the Mind," *Scientific American* 301, no. 3 (September 2009): 44–51.

16. Marc Hauser, "Origin of the Mind," 45–46.

17. Available online at http://www.vatican.va/holy_father/pius_xii/encyclicals/documents/hf_p-xii_enc_12081950_humani-generis_en.html Accessed 8 November, 2010.

18. For readers interested in this connection, see Cardinal Christoph Schönborn's magnificent *God's Human Face: the Christ-Icon* (San Francisco, CA: Ignatius, 1994), trans. Lothar Krauth.

19. On this connection between our intellectual capacities and the conditions of knowability pertaining in nature see my *A*

Meaningful World, Denton's *Nature's Destiny*, and most of all, Gonzalez and Richard's *Privileged Planet*.

20. Pope Benedict XVI, Meeting with the Representatives of Science Lecture of The Holy Father, Aula Magna of the University of Regensburg, Tuesday, September 12, 2006, "Faith, Reason and the University Memories and Reflections," accessed November 8, 2010, http://www.vatican.va/holy _father/benedict_xvi/speeches/2006/september/documents/ hf_benxvi_spe_20060912_university-regensburg_en.html.

Chapter 7

1. This chapter is adapted from the article, Benjamin Wiker, "Alien Ideas: Christianity and the Search for Extraterrestrial Life" from the November 2002 issue of *Crisis Magazine*.

2. According to the reports of Hippolytus. See G. S. Kirk and J. E. Raven, *The Presocratic Philosophers: A Critical History with a Selection of Texts* (Cambridge: Cambridge University Press, 1960), section 564, p. 411.

3. Epicurus, "Letter to Herodotus," in *The Epicurus Reader*, trans. and ed. Brad Inwood and L. P. Gerson, paragraph 45, p. 8.

4. Lucretius, *On the Nature of the Universe*, translated by R. E. Latham (New York: Penguin, 1994), Book Five, Lines 186–90.

5. Lucretius, *On the Nature of the Universe*, Book Two, Lines 1051–58, 1066–77, 1090–92. The emphasis is from the translator, but one must admit, the points are well worth emphasizing.

6. Aristotle, *Physics*, 260a20–267b26; *On Generation and Corruption*, 336a15–337a7.

7. Quoted in Michael Crowe, *The Extraterrestrial Life Debate, 1750–1900* (Mineola, NY: Dover, 1999), 8.

8. Quoted in Crowe, *The Extraterrestrial Life Debate, 1750–1900*, 8.

9. Quoted in Crowe, *The Extraterrestrial Life Debate, 1750–1900*, 8–9.

10. Quoted in Crowe, *The Extraterrestrial Life Debate, 1750–1900*, 23.

11. See Crowe, *The Extraterrestrial Life Debate, 1750–1900*, 31–33.

12. Crowe, *The Extraterrestrial Life Debate, 1750–1900*, 169.

13. Crowe, *The Extraterrestrial Life Debate, 1750–1900*, 170.

14. Crowe, *The Extraterrestrial Life Debate, 1750–1900*, 48–53.

15. Crowe, *The Extraterrestrial Life Debate, 1750–1900*, 255.

16. Crowe, *The Extraterrestrial Life Debate, 1750–1900*, 67.

17. Crowe, *The Extraterrestrial Life Debate, 1750–1900*, 73.

18. Crowe, *The Extraterrestrial Life Debate, 1750–1900*, 249.

19. Crowe, *The Extraterrestrial Life Debate, 1750–1900*, 135.

20. Crowe, *The Extraterrestrial Life Debate, 1750–1900*, 99.

21. Crowe, *The Extraterrestrial Life Debate, 1750–1900*, 238.

22. Crowe, *The Extraterrestrial Life Debate, 1750–1900*, 239–40.

23. Crowe, *The Extraterrestrial Life Debate, 1750–1900*, 244.

24. Crowe, *The Extraterrestrial Life Debate, 1750–1900*, 163.

25. Crowe, The *Extraterrestrial Life Debate, 1750–1900,* chap. 6.

26. On SETI, see Steven Dick in *Life on Other Worlds: The 20th-Century Extraterrestrial Life Debate* (Cambridge: Cambridge University Press, 1998), chap. 7.

27. See SETI's website: http://www.seti.org/Page.aspx?pid=1366

28. I don't wish to imply that a person of great faith may not ponder the questions surrounding the possibility of alien life. One of Christianity's great apologists, C. S. Lewis, wrote three masterpieces of science fiction, known collectively as the Space Trilogy. This imaginative inquiry into what alien life might be like and how it would relate to Christian salvation is, however, a great exception: everything in the three books, *Out of the Silent Planet, Perelandra,* and *That Hideous Strength,* is entirely bent toward Christian orthodoxy. Also, if I recall correctly, after writing the trilogy, and getting such speculation out of his system, Lewis dropped the whole notion of

ETs as foolish. But my larger point is that, again, Lewis's overriding concern for Christian orthodoxy is the rare exception rather than the rule. Something like Mormonism is the rule.

29. For a report, see http://www.catholicnewsagency.com/news/believing_in_aliens_not_opposed_to_christianity_vaticans_top_astronomer_says/, accessed November 8, 2010.

30. A report of the interview can be found at http://www.catholicnewsagency.com/news/believing_in_aliens_not_opposed_to_christianity_vaticans_top_astronomer_says/, accessed November 8, 2010.

Conclusion

1. Pope Benedict XVI, General Audience, March 24, 2010. Available on the Vatican website at http://www.vatican.va/holy_father/benedict_xvi/audiences/2010/documents/hf_ben-xvi_aud_20100324_en.html

About the Author

BENJAMIN WIKER received his Ph.D. in Theological Ethics from Vanderbilt University. He is the author of eight previous books, including *Ten Books Every Conservative Must Read* (Regnery), *Answering the New Atheism* (with Scott Hahn, Emmaus), and *A Meaningful World* (with Jonathan Witt, IVP). Dr. Wiker is a Senior Fellow with the Envoy Institute of Belmont Abbey College, a Senior Fellow with the St. Paul Center for Biblical Theology, and a Senior Fellow with Discovery Institute. He has a new radio show called A Meaningful World. He lives with his beloved wife and children in rural Ohio.